Battleground Europe
OPERATION

MW00528930

HELL'S HIGHWAY

Cover painting by James Dietz, WRATH OF THE RED DEVILS, Operation Market Garden, September, 1944.

Battleground Europe
OPERATION MARKET GARDEN

HELL'S HIGHWAY

Tim Saunders

LEO COOPER

*To my son William Saunders
with love*

Published by
LEO COOPER
an imprint of
Pen & Sword Books Limited
47 Church Street, Barnsley, South Yorkshire S70 2AS
Copyright © Tim Saunders 2001

ISBN 0 85052 837 2

A CIP record of this book is available
from the British Library

Printed in the United Kingdom by
CPI UK

*For up-to-date information on other titles produced under the Leo Cooper
imprint, please telephone or write to:*

Pen & Sword Books Ltd, FREEPOST SF5, 47 Church Street
Barnsley, South Yorkshire S70 2BR
Telephone 01226 734555

CONTENTS

ACKNOWLEDGEMENTS

I am indebted to veterans on both sides of the Atlantic, particularly those of 101st Airborne Division, for their help in preparing this book. Much has been written over the fifty years since the dramatic events of September 1944. However, much of the material has proved to be superficial, contradictory and often simply incorrect but veterans' contributions and examination of archives have helped clear up a number of issues and myths. Again, I am indebted to the hard-pressed staff of the regimental headquarters of the British units, whose forebears' battles are covered in this book. They have been most helpful, overworked regimental secretaries or highly knowledgeable volunteers have been a mine of information and guidance. Across the Atlantic, veterans' associations have helped me with official and personal accounts. Visits to the Public Record Office and airborne museums in Britain and Holland to view their archives were essential and I unreservedly thank them for their help.

I would like to thank the many Dutch people who helped me locate and gain access to some of the more obscure sites and for providing me with numerous maps and photographs. It would take too long to name them here but their greatest contribution has been their warmth and friendliness. Sources in Germany, have helped guide me to records of *Wehrmacht* and *Luftwaffe* units, including to some of the many *ad hoc* formations and units taking part in the fighting on Hell's Highway

Again, I am indebted to both family and friends for their tolerant support and encouragement, while I researched and wrote this book. I am most grateful for the time they spent spotting my errors and inconsistencies, while reading through all too many drafts of the manuscript. Thank you one and all.

Tim Saunders
Lichfield, Staffs

INTRODUCTION

This volume of the *Battleground Europe* series starts with one of the most celebrated events of the North West-European Campaign, the spectacular capture of Joe's Bridge by the Irish Guards. Though, strictly, not a part of MARKET GARDEN, it is an important and exciting precursor. This is followed by an explanation of the controversial and optimistic assumptions made by 21st Army Group and the Airborne Army's planning staff and the difficult logistic and Alliance issues that General Eisenhower had to deal with. However, the meat of the book covers the part played in operation MARKET GARDEN by 101st US Airborne and the British Guards Armoured Divisions in the heady days of September 1944, following the German defeat in Normandy. The first phase of the battle was the seizure of the river and canal bridges on twenty miles of road between the city of Eindhoven and the town of Veghel. The British XXX Corps were to drive north up the road, variously called the 'Corridor', 'Centre Line' or 'Club Route' and the Americans, with full justification, came to know as Hell's Highway. Over the following days, in operations reminiscent of the Indian Wars fought on the Great Plains of America, the 101st Airborne or 'Screaming Eagles' marched and counter-marched to keep German *Kampfgruppen* at bay.

Almost without exception, accounts of MARKET GARDEN correctly stress the difficulties of moving across country. However, in most cases the difficulties were not of becoming instantly bogged down in 'wet going' but of crossing the many drainage ditches, encountering weak bridges and a fear of anti-tank mines. Tanks could and indeed did take short excursions

across country but they were invariably very slow.

During MARKET GARDEN, the Germans displayed their ability to mount an effective defence with *ad hoc* formations of units and individuals who, in this case, had escaped from the German fortresses along the North Sea coast. In retrospect, the failure to secure the sixty-mile Scheldt waterway between Antwerp and the sea, across which the Germans escaped, was a grievous error. These escapees, augmented by trainees from what was a rear area, were able to pose a significant threat to the pencil thin Hell's Highway. But for the tough and experienced paratroopers of 101st Airborne Division, and their attached British armour, the Germans may have succeeded in inflicting a crushing reverse on an extremely exposed British 2nd Army.

It should be borne in mind that, while 101st and elements of the Guards Armoured Divisions were fighting on Hell's Highway, further to the north, others were fighting equally desperate battles. The fighting by British and American troops in the Nijmegen/Groesbeek area, on The Island (between the Waal and the Rhine) and at Arnhem, is covered in separate *Battleground* volumes.

As a final point, I would like to explain that I have covered the principal memorials in the battle area. However, space has not permitted me to include details and photographs of every memorial to the 101st and every community's memorial to its liberation. However, they can be easily found in town centres or at the scene of the action described in the following chapters.

I hope this book will encourage those studying MARKET GARDEN to visit and appreciate the highly significant battles fought on Hell's Highway, the road to Arnhem.

At home or on the ground, enjoy the tour.

German troops intent on withdrawing from the North Sea coast.

ADVICE TO VISITORS

Travel to Holland

A range of ferry crossings to mainland Europe and Holland are available from various UK ports, that can be used by those visiting the MARKET GARDEN battlefields. In the north, Newcastle has an overnight service (fourteen hours) to Amsterdam and further south, Hull has a similar service to Zeebrugge. Harwich has sailings to the Hook of Holland (three and a half hours). Both Amsterdam and the Hook are about two hours drive from Eindoven, on good motorways. Sailings from the East Coast are not as frequent and can be more costly than those from the Channel Ports but savings in fuel and tiredness always make East Coast services worth considering. The Channel crossing, though shorter and quicker, do mean that the visitor is faced with a three to four-hour drive from Calais, via busy motorways (toll-free) around Antwerp and through southern Holland. For those who dislike ferries there is the Channel Tunnel, but this option, though quicker, is usually more expensive. It is worth checking out all the options available and make your selection of route based on UK travel, ferry times and cost. Special offers and Internet deals are always worth keeping an eye on and have, in my case, resulted in *impromptu* visits to the Continental battlefields.

Traffic law requires drivers to carry a full driving licence, a vehicle registration document, warning triangle and a spare fuel can of an approved type. Spare head light bulbs etc should be taken and, if your headlights do not have left-hand drive adapters, black tape. Do not forget your passport and a GB sticker. A good web site to visit for up to date travel information is http://www.visitholland.com/geninfo/travel/.

Insurance

It is important to check that all visitors are properly insured to travel in France, Belgium and Holland. Firstly, check with insurance brokers to ensure that your car is properly covered for driving in the above countries and, secondly, make sure all have health cover. It is a legal requirement for a driver to carry a valid certificate of motor insurance. For those travelling by air and hiring cars, Amsterdam/Schipol is a major international hub, while Eindhoven is a significant regional airport in the centre of the Hell's Highway battle area. For EU Citizens, form E111, available from post offices, grants the bearer reciprocal treatment rights in most European countries. However, the visitor should give serious consideration to purchasing a package of travel insurance from a broker or travel agent.

Accommodation

The Hell's Highway battle area is dominated by the vastly expanded city of Eindhoven. Those who are drawn to cities will find every grade of hotel in the city but during weekdays it is advisable to book in advance, as rooms fill up with business travellers. The towns on the route, Valkenswaard, Son en Brugel, St Oedenrode, Veghel and Uden, all have attractive hotels of varying styles and grade. There are also significant numbers of well-ordered campsites, which represent good value for money and offer a wide range of services. Information on availability of rooms and bookings can be supplied by the Dutch Tourist Office. For those with access to the Internet, a visit to the following web site will be helpful if searching for the better hotels:

http:/hotels.bookings.nl/tourist.nederland.hotbot.html/.

For those who wish to combine a family holiday with a tour of Hell's Highway, a CentreParcs complex is located at Valkenswaard.

Courtesy

Despite considerable expansion of the villages, towns and cities on Hell's Highway, much of the battle-area covered in this book, is open farmland, with many of the villages forming important parts of the battlefield. Whether open country or built up area, please respect private property, particularly avoid driving on unmade up farm tracks and entering non-public areas in villages. Adequate views of the scene of the action can be enjoyed from public land. Drivers should be particularly aware of the many cyclists in this flat part of Holland and please watch out for cycle lanes, which should not be blocked by careless parking. The people of Holland extend a genuine welcome to those who come to honour the memory of their Allied liberators. To preserve this welcome, please bear in mind the local people.

Maps

Good maps are an essential prerequisite to a successful battlefield visit. Best of all is a combination of contemporary and modern maps. The Battleground series of course, provides wartime maps, however, a full modern map sheet enables the visitor or those who are exploring the battlefield from the comfort of their armchair, to put the battle in a wider context. A number of modern maps are available in both the UK and Holland. A good road map of Holland is essential to navigate around Hell's Highway, which takes the visitor on to some minor roads. The best and most detailed map coverage is available from stationers in Eindhoven. In the UK, detailed maps of the Netherlands are normally only available on order from a specialist map shop or as a special order through high street bookshops such as Waterstones.

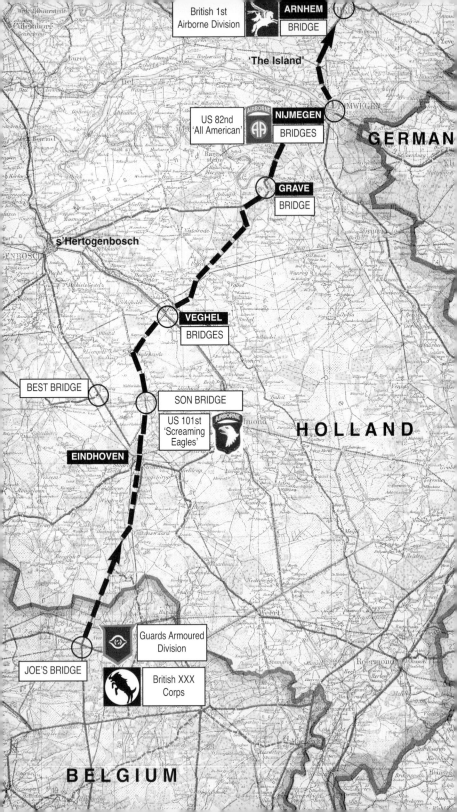

British 1st
Airborne Division

ARNHEM

BRIDGE

'The Island'

US 82nd
'All American'

NIJMEGEN

BRIDGES

GERMAN

GRAVE

BRIDGE

s'Hertogenbosch

VEGHEL

BRIDGES

BEST BRIDGE

SON BRIDGE

US 101st
'Screaming
Eagles'

HOLLAND

EINDHOVEN

Guards Armoured
Division

British XXX
Corps

JOE'S BRIDGE

BELGIUM

CHAPTER ONE

JOE'S BRIDGE
The Irish Guards seize a vital bridge

After D Day, the Allies initially made slow progress in terms of captured terrain, with the SHAEF planners' expectations not being met. However, by mid August, after some hard fighting the Germans collapsed into defeat. The Normandy Campaign was won and the German defeat, when it came, was as complete as was Montgomery's victory over his many critics. The remnants of the German Seventh Army streamed eastwards. The Germans attempted to halt the Allies on the Seine (reached fifteen days ahead of Montgomery's pre-D-Day prediction) and, subsequently, on the River Somme. However, the Allied armoured divisions' momentum was such that each obstacle was 'bounced' and the advance continued, at rates of up to fifty miles a day. The contrast between the hard slogging of the Normandy battles and the swift advances served only to sharpen in the minds of both commanders and front-line soldiers, the prospect that the war was almost over.

As the British armoured divisions swept across northern France and Belgium, Allied commanders, attempted to convince Eisenhower that their approach to Germany offered the best way to victory. However, the further the widely scattered units moved from their logistic base in Normandy the harder it was to sustain such spectacular advances. At the same time, as they approached the Reich, German resistance perceptibly stiffened, with northern Belgium's numerous waterways providing many defensive opportunities

Brussels fell to the Guards Armoured Division without a serious fight on 3 September 1944. A day later, the vital port of Antwerp fell into the hands of 11th Armoured Division with its facilities intact. However, in the euphoria, the commanders of the thinly spread troops overlooked the clearance of the sixty mile Scheldt Estuary that gave access to Antwerp. This omission also provided an escape route for the outflanked Germans who were 'trapped' along the Channel coast. As we shall see, the escape of these troops was to have a profound effect on the

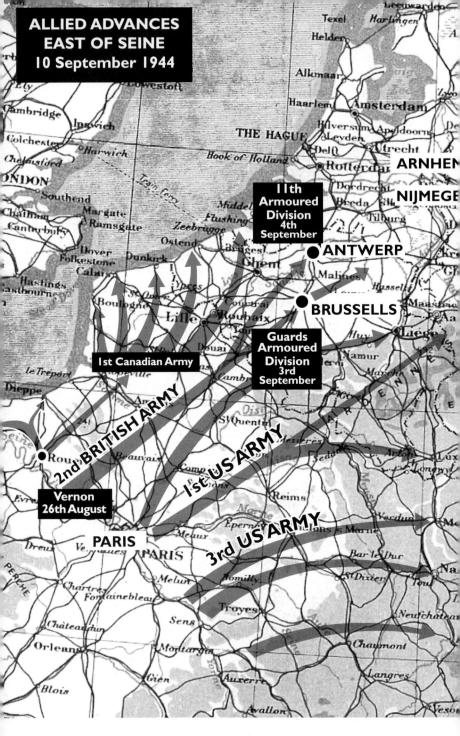

ALLIED ADVANCES
EAST OF SEINE
10 September 1944

11th Armoured Division 4th September

Guards Armoured Division 3rd September

1st Canadian Army

2nd BRITISH ARMY

1st US ARMY

3rd US ARMY

Vernon 26th August

PARIS

ANTWERP

BRUSSELLS

ARNHEM

NIJMEGE

14

outcome of Operation MARKET GARDEN. Meanwhile, the advance of the Guards continued eastwards, albeit more slowly than before.

The tour of Hell's Highway starts at the De Groote Barrier.

Take the E313 from the **Antwerp Ring** and after approximately thirty kilometres turn off towards **Geel** on the N71. Stay on the road through **Lommel**. After three kilometres turn left on to the **N715** following the signs to **Lommel Barrier** (the modern name for the area of De Grote Barrier/Joe's Bridge). A Polish War Cemetery dating from the post MARKET GARDEN period is on the left. Continue straight on to **Barrier**. The factory chimneys and buildings featured in this chapter

Joe's Bridge and the view of the factory to the south east.

can be seen half right. The cafes and bars of the small village centre that stands around the crossroads make a good spot for refreshment before the tour begins. The first stand is across the bridge. Cross the modern steel bridge that has long-since replaced the wooden trestle affair that the Germans built after the 1940 campaign. Once across the bridge, take the first turning left (**Luiersteenweg**) and double back down to the canal towpath. Park opposite the house at the end of the road. All of the significant action can be seen or easily understood from the area of the bridge. A small memorial to the Irish Guards is located on the other side of the ramp.

Seizure of the de Groote Bridge

On 10 September 1944, the Guards Armoured Division, spearhead of 2nd Army, was advancing on a five-mile frontage from the Beringen bridgehead towards the Escaut Canal, with armoured cars of A Squadron, 2nd Household Cavalry Regiment (2/HCR) leading. Against significant enemy opposition, 2/HCR's mission was to locate the enemy and identify routes but, above all, they were to find a suitable point to cross the Escaut Canal. Ideally, the crossing should be a bridge seized intact, as the divisional engineers had been only able to carry limited bridging stores with them. However, a

Armoured cars of the 2nd Household Cavalry driving through Holland.

JOES BRIDGE

INFANTRY ASSAULT

ARMOURED FOLLOW-UP

CROSS ROADS

partly blown bridge that could be repaired with the available resources, was acceptable. Complicating matters, was the fact that the advance had been so rapid that the Guards had out-run their map coverage and, consequently, a small-scale road or school map became a prized possession. However, such maps gave few details and the Household Cavalry were, as a result,

feeling their way forward trying to identify routes around enemy positions suitable for the tanks of their division. German resistance was stiff and the difficult country did not help progress, which was slow.

By afternoon, Lieutenant Creswell's troop of 2/HCR were pushing on towards the Escaut Canal and found a newly constructed and undefended road that was not marked on their road maps. More importantly it by-passed the enemy. He wrote:

17

'I was well aware of the opposition which was being experienced by the Grenadier Group on the main road, for several 'A' Squadron Troops were also engaged there and I could hear their reports on the wireless. For this reason I could not bring myself to believe that the enemy would be so foolish as to leave an alternative route uncovered, and in fact I stressed in my orders to the Troop the fact that we must expect opposition. Never the less, although we drove tactically and with due caution, we covered a distance of twelve kilometres to within three kilometres of the bridge at de Groote Barrier, having seen but one German standing in a field and demanding to be taken prisoner.'

Cautiously closing in on the Escaut Canal, having outflanked the enemy, the bridge was approached via the canal bank. German built it was a high level, wooden trestle type, replacing that blown by the Belgians in 1940. Lieutenant Creswell realized that his armoured cars would be seen if he advanced any further but a large factory ahead offered the possibility of observing the bridge. So, in the gathering dusk, amongst a growing crowd of cheering Belgians *'I borrowed two bicycles and, leaving the Troop in command of Corporal Corton, set off to the factory with Corporal-of-Horse* [Household Cavalry equivalent of a sergeant] *Cutler'*. To the hastily hushed applause of the locals, the spearhead of 2nd British Army set off on their bikes. The Regimental Historian describes what happened:

'The outward journey was accomplished successfully, although just before reaching the factory an enemy patrol was seen on the other side of the canal, and in moving out of sight, Corporal-of-Horse Culter, who admitted that he was more at home in the turret of a Daimler than at the wheel of a Belgian racing bicycle, toppled off the machine, his Sten gun clattering on the road. Fortunately, like the cheering, the mishap went unnoticed.

Leaving the bicycles outside the factory, and with a Belgian caretaker acting as lookout, Creswell and Cutler climbed to the top of the building, where the former by dint of pushing his head through a skylight, could clearly see the bridge. ... Beneath him lay the whole plan of the enemy's defences, spread out as if marked upon an overprint map.'

Lieutenant Creswell was able to note down his recommended approaches to the bridge, before a burst of machine gun fire

The original abutments where the Germans had placed their demolition circuits.

caused him to abandon his excellent OP. The two Household Cavalrymen returned to their armoured cars and radioed the information back to the Guards Armoured Division. At 18.30 hours, XXX Corps received word that '2/HCR report, br 3596 all right but strongly held.' Both the Grenadier Guards and the Irish Guards Group, some eight miles to their rear, were tasked to go for the bridge. The Grenadiers were, however, held up on the main road but Lieutenant Colonel JOE Vandeleur with 3/IG (infantry), 2/IG (tanks) and a troop of Honey light tanks, was on an open eastern flank. He led No. 1 Squadron, accompanied by the infantry of No.2 Company, forward via the new road and halting his tanks well away from the bridge, he went forward to make a plan.

Climbing a slagheap with the Squadron Leader Major David Peel, Colonel 'Joe' could see that the enemy had concentrated his defences on the northern bank around the bridge. Three deadly 88mm guns, taken from airfield defence in Holland, formed the core of the German position and numerous infantrymen lounged around their sandbagged trenches, leaning on their Spandaus. Colonel Vandeleur could see that he had a problem. His lightly armoured Sherman tanks were extremely vulnerable to the 88mm and his infantry would be cut down by the machine guns in a direct attack. So fast had the advance been, he was also out of radio contact with his brigade headquarters and the artillery. He was on his own but the bridge had to be taken. He concluded that 'Obviously boldness is the thing. We will rush the bridge'. This minimized the enemy's chances of blowing the bridge as his tanks and infantry approached and would keep casualties to a minimum. His plan was that:

'David Peel's squadron was to send one troop of tanks, commanded by Duncan Lampard, to the corner of the curve. This was to be accompanied by a platoon of the 3rd Battalion, commanded by John Stanley-Clarke, which was to be the assault force, with Michael Dudley's Company and the remainder of David Peel's squadron engaging the enemy point-blank with fire for twenty minutes.'

Accompanying the Irish Guards was their Royal Engineer troop commander, Captain Hutton, but being far ahead of his Troop's main body, he was also unable to contact them by radio. As the sole representative of his Corps, along with his radio operator Sapper Davies and his batman, Sapper Smith, the task of removing the German demolition charges would fall to him. Summoned by Colonel Vandeleur he was briefed on the plan.

'I am going to charge the bridge with a troop of tanks. I want you to go with them and make sure the thing's safe. I replied that "I don't have any Sappers with me and I have no technical details of the bridge." Whereupon four weary guardsmen were called for from the side of the road, and that was that! None of whom had the slightest idea about demolition technique - especially of the German variety. I split my men up into two parties, one of which, under Davies, was to cut all wires and any likely looking things they could find under the near end of the bridge, Smith and his two men were to do the same at the far end, I was to look for and destroy the electrical circuit. The bridge like all canal bridges, was very high and anyone crossing it would be silhouetted against the sky, whilst the approach road sloped steeply, making surprise very difficult'

At 20.00 hours, the two tanks that were going to charge the bridge, preceded by the infantry, made their way towards the bridge along the main road under covering fire of the other

Shermans from the area of the factory. As the covering fire started, an 88mm gun on the southern side of the canal that had not been identified during the reconnaissance was knocked out. Its half-track towing and ammunition tractor attempted to dash across the bridge. Captain Hutton recalls that the vehicle was knocked out on the bridge and how in the gathering darkness:

> 'The exploding shells made the attack even more hazardous, while the flames lit the whole area of the bridge, and doubtless added to the confusion of the defenders. Three other 88mm guns were positioned near at hand covering the northern end of the bridge, supported by infantry with Spandaus, who fired almost continuous bursts, whilst over our heads and to our right, the supporting tanks poured out a curtain of fire.'

Meanwhile, the infantry had worked their way forward to the bend in the approach road, about a hundred metres south of the bridge, and they fired a green Verey light to initiate the main attack. The Irishmen dashed forward followed by the two tanks under a crescendo of covering fire from eleven tanks of No. 1 Squadron. In a matter of moments a red Verey light cut an arc through the night sky, indicating that the infantry had reached the far side and that the tanks should charge across the bridge to join them. Crashing through the burning wreckage the Shermans were across. Despite the lack of artillery support, the formidable firepower of a tank squadron at short-range against the surprised *Luftwaffe* soldiers of the Herman Goring Division, was sufficient to ensure success. Dashing behind the tanks was Captain Hutton and his small group of Sappers and

JOE'S BRIDGE

IRISH GUARDS

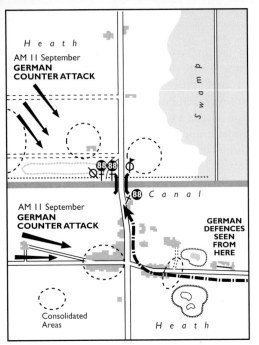

Heath

AM 11 September
**GERMAN
COUNTER ATTACK**

Swamp

88 88

Canal

AM 11 September
**GERMAN
COUNTER ATTACK**

88

**GERMAN
DEFENCES
SEEN
FROM
HERE**

Consolidated
Areas

Heath

Guardsmen.

'On reaching the bridge... I discovered that the side of the road were covered by a confusion of wires, fuses, etc, of every description, easily visible in the light of the burning ammunition truck and the sporadic shell bursts. Having shot through everything I could find with my revolver, as the wire cutters had by now fallen into the canal, I ran back, causing some consternation amongst the second wave of assaulting infantry to see how Davies was getting on.

A towpath ran under the near side of the bridge, and on this I found my three men still cutting detonating fuse. There were twelve ANZ 29 switches hanging from the wall, two forming alternate initiating sets for the complete demolition and ten running to individual charges on the home abutment and the two nearest trestles... Also on the towpath were two Germans, one quite dead and the second suffering considerable pain from a severed right leg. Were these part of the firing party? - we never found out.

Once I had made sure all the initiating assemblies had been removed from the charges, I climbed onto the bridge, where I met "Colonel Joe" running across to join the assaulting troops, and, having reported that the bridge was safe and arranged for guards, I returned to my truck, parked thoughtfully by Trendall beside the nearby café, for a much needed drink.'

The attack was spectacularly successful and casualties were much lighter than could have been reasonably expected, with only three men wounded. Colonel Joe had combined surprise with effective fire and manoeuvre, the whole plan being executed with considerable Irish elan. Apparently, the Germans were taken totally by surprise. So surprised were they that key and hitherto well-respected members of the garrison, such as the officer in command of the bridge's explosive demolition firing party, ran as the Micks deluged the bridge with fire. The German bridge demolition guard had been kept informed about the battle on the main road well to their front and the thought that the blocking force could have been so daringly outflanked, had seemingly not entered their minds. Consequently, they believed that the not inconsiderable noise of a squadron of Shermans was that of their own armour. One German prisoner slapped an Irish Guards officer on the back and said 'Well done Tommy, well done!'

While Captain Hutton gratefully recovered in the café from the tension of successfully defusing a primed bridge demolition of 2,000 pounds of explosive, Lieutenant Colonel JOE Vandeleur set about preparing the defence of the bridge.

> 'I formed a minimum bridgehead and a squadron of tanks on
> the north bank and prepared the position for all-round defence. It
> was obvious that the Germans would try to recapture the bridge
> and in all probability from the rear. A large number of German
> troops had been cut off from their line of retreat and they were
> not going to take this lying down.'

The Irish Guards were still out of radio contact with their commanders some fifteen miles to their rear but Lieutenant Creswell was able to get through to his colonel who was co-located with

1st Dorset crossing Joe's Bridge into the new bridgehead after its capture.

Major General Adair. Not expecting such dramatic news, Headquarters Guards Armoured Division demanded independent confirmation of the bridge's capture but once convinced, they wanted to exploit success and push the whole of 5 Guards Brigade across. However, Headquarters XXX Corps countermanded the order, as many Germans had been bypassed in the ten-mile advance from the Albert Canal to the Escaut Canal and there was a very real possibility that 5 Guards Brigade would be cut off by denuding the area south of the bridgehead of troops. Consequently, only one squadron of tanks and two companies of infantry held the bridgehead, when the inevitable enemy counter-attacks came in at dawn the following morning. Major David Peel was killed, beating off the counter-attacks and, as is often the case a daring coup de main force, having achieved its aim at little cost, finds holding on to its gains far more costly. David Peel won a well-deserved Military Cross for taking the bridge on the night of 10 September 1944.

Lieutenant General Horrocks wrote of his visit to the Irish guards the following day:

> 'I was so impressed with Vandeleur's brilliant and inspiring leadership that I gave orders for the De Groot Bridge to be called "Joe's Bridge"... and as such it will always be remembered in the annals of the British Army.' As an opening move to a new phase of the North West European Campaign, the seizure of Joe's Bridge by armoured troops was every bit as important and competently executed as the capture of Pegasus Bridge three months earlier. During his visit, General Horrocks told the Irish Guards that their success had made the next stage of the campaign easier and that they would have the honour of leading the next push. In an unusually candid remark for a regimental history, the Irish Guards' author recorded that "This last remark took the gilt off the gingerbread".'

As has been pointed out many times before, experienced soldiers are not keen on getting shot – even for a good or heroic cause!

Lieutenant Buchanan-Jardine's Recce - 11 September 1944

Although those at the front did not appreciate it at the time, Joe's Bridge and its small bridgehead was vital to Montgomery's future plans. Of almost as much significance, was the next bridge, which crossed the River Dommel just south

of Valkenswaard. 2/HCR were tasked to report on its state and
how well it was defended. The words of Lieutenant General
Horrocks, the Corps Commander, can best describe what
happened to Lieutenant Buchanan-Jardine's troop of D
Squadron.

'My first problem was to find out the nature of the enemy's
defences opposed to our bridgehead, which had widened to a
depth of approximately 3-5 miles. The German forces in front of

German prisoners are led away from the area after the unsuccessful counter-attack to retake the bridge.

us were paratroopers, and more were appearing every day. I wanted to find out just how deep were their defences, and whether the bridge over the River Dommel, leading to the first little Dutch town of Valkenswaard, was still intact and strong enough to take tanks. This was obviously a job for the Household Cavalry [the Corps' recce regiment], who I expected would find a way round as usual, but this proved impossible as the country in front of us was thick, wooded and mined. The highly dangerous and difficult job of obtaining the vital information for the next move forward was handed over to the troop commanded by Lieutenant Buchanan-Jardine, who realized very soon that the only thing to do was to bluff his way through. He therefore left behind his two armoured cars which were certain to be destroyed, and decided to drive his two scout cars flat out straight down the one main central road, right through the enemy positions. This he did, encountering numerous enemy defences on the way; but the two little Daimlers roared on, nothing daunted, and their speed carried them through. By 2 p.m. they were well inside the Netherlands and stopped at a small café, from where the bridge could be seen. They were now clear of the defences and reported this fact by wireless. They also saw a German Mark IV crossing the bridge, so we knew that it was strong enough to take tanks.

No sooner had they arrived than a band of overjoyed Dutch surrounded them, shouting and slapping them on their backs, making noise enough to attract the attention of any German within miles. Buchanan-Jardine warned them that this was not the Liberation - that would come later. It was only a reconnaissance. He obtained from them much valuable information, all of which was wirelessed back. Now came the problem of his return. There was only one thing for it - the two little cars once more set out through the German lines, flat out again, with everything firing at them. Nose to tail they raced back and got through to our lines. Everything on the outside of the cars was punctured and broken by small arms fire - including even the precious cooking utensils. Sad to relate, they

2nd Devon moving forward to the bridgehead across Joe's Bridge.

learned later from a Dutchman that after their departure the Germans had gone to the Café and shot three civilians in cold blood.'

The Irish Guards were surprised to see the two armoured vehicles racing back across No Man's Land, engines screaming at the unaccustomed speed of over sixty miles an hour but the Guards were as good as their parting words 'we promise we won't shoot you up, **if** you return'.

Lieutenant Buchanan-Jardine, along with his driver, Trooper Buckley, was the first Allied soldier to enter the Netherlands and was awarded the Bronze Lion of the Netherlands and a well deserved Military Cross. Thanks to his courage and dash, his information confirmed to XXX Corps that breaking through the German positions, which were four miles in depth was possible. During the recce they had passed through the main position and through no less than three infantry positions – twice and survived to tell the tale. It was clear that any attack up this road was not going to be easy and XXX Corps knew that the Germans were growing in strength with every day that passed.

The Germans were beginning to react to the initial incursions towards the Belgian – Dutch border.

CHAPTER TWO

BACKGROUND AND THE MARKET GARDEN PLAN
Alliance Politics, logistics and Montgomery's plan

General Omar Bradley

'Had the pious teetotalling Monty wobbled into SHAEF with a hangover, I could not have been more astonished than I was by the daring adventure he proposed!'
General Omar Bradley

It is not within this book's scope to provide a detailed analysis of Operation MARKET GARDEN's controversial background. This short chapter, is a résumé of the factors, political and military, that shaped Montgomery's plan. However, it is in sufficient detail for MARKET GARDEN to be seen in the context of the North West European Campaign as a whole.

Alliance Politics

General Eisenhower assumed conduct of the campaign from Field Marshal Montgomery on 1 September 1944. The extent of the Allied victory and the speed of the advance eastwards eclipsed SHAEF's ability to plan and left Eisenhower lacking a detailed strategy when he took full command. Eisenhower has been criticised as not being a decisive commander but, after Normandy, there was no shortage of plans being advanced by his generals and, at one stage, it seemed as if he was agreeing to support all of them. However, Eisenhower's problem in selecting a strategy was extremely difficult, as British and American plans were no longer subject to the common goal of defeating a powerful enemy and his generals' personal ambitions had become pre-eminent. With such difficult characters as Patton and Montgomery and their respective press corps to deal with, Eisenhower's command was not easy and

The Supreme Commander, General Eisenhower appears to be paying close attention as Montgomery 'bends his ear'.

the Supreme Commander was working primarily at a political level. Whatever the arguments in favour of Montgomery's narrow front advance into Germany, it would never be acceptable to US public opinion to have Patton's Third Army halted, with the 'victor's laurels' going to Montgomery. It is clear that Eisenhower found considerable favour with the arguments for the northern route to Berlin but political realities forced him to adopt the 'attack everywhere' philosophy that underpinned the US broad front strategy of the day.

Other than his generals' prestige and national pride, Eisenhower had other pressing factors to consider as he made his decisions on 7 September 1944. Firstly, after five years of war, Britain was at the end of her resources and the European war needed to be over by Christmas 1944. Secondly, V2 ballistic missiles, launched from north-west Holland, were falling on London. The need to clear the enemy from the launch sites, thus take the missiles out of range, was one of Churchill's key requirements. Thirdly, another European factor was that Churchill did not want the Soviets in the heart of Europe and, therefore, being the first to Berlin was important. Fourthly, the Ruhr industrial area, despite the Strategic Bomber Offensive, was still the powerhouse of Germany and in 1944, tank production rose to a record 19,002 vehicles. It was estimated that capturing the Ruhr Triangle would end the war within three months. As the Supreme Commander formulated his plan, these factors had to be balanced and considered.

In coming to his decision, the Supreme Commander pleased none of his 'difficult' subordinate commanders. This is illustrated by Patton's comment that Eisenhower was 'the best general the British have' and indicates that Eisenhower was even-handed. Another prophetic quote from Patton in that year, 1944, summed up Eisenhower's politic role in the European campaign; 'he'd make a better president than a general'.

George S. Patton did not see eye-to-eye with Montgomery and was critical of his superior.

Logistics

Logistics lay at the heart of Eisenhower's political and military problems: in early September, he could not sustain even a half of his forces in offensive operations at any one time. The rapid advance had taken his armies two hundred and fifty miles from their supply bases. Still without a major port in operation, his armies were largely supplied through the artificial Mulberry harbour and across the Normandy beaches. Commanders were prepared to lobby hard, for all the supplies that they could get. Typically, they would paint an over-optimistic picture of the prospects on their front in order to secure additional resources: General Patton is widely acknowledged as the master of this technique. However, the further the front advanced eastwards, the fewer troops were able to pursue the Germans. Infantry divisions were 'grounded' and their trucks stripped from them to transport combat supplies needed to keep the armoured divisions mobile. Fewer troops at the front meant a reduction in combat power and they also had to cover wider frontages. Consequently, there was an increasing likelihood of *ad hoc* German defences halting the advancing Allies. To make the situation worse, Allied soldiers were increasingly unlikely to risk their lives in what they perceived to be the final weeks of the war.

First Allied Airborne Army

Airborne forces had been embraced by the US Army prior to the war and, following their successful use by the Germans in 1940, the British formed their first airborne units later that year. By 1944, airborne forces were sufficiently strong to warrant grouping into their own Army, with a headquarters to look after their interests. Considerable resources, as strategic bomber commanders saw it, had been diverted into transport aircraft to support the new arm. The First Allied Airborne Army was also Eisenhower's only strategic reserve, contrary to the impression that the Germans still held as a result of the deception operation; FORTITUDE. In addition, the US Chief of Staff, General Marshall, was pressing Eisenhower to find a use for this expensive asset, as the airborne divisions were *'coins burning holes in SHAEF's pocket'*. Attempts had been made to utilise 1st (British) Airborne Division but the speed of the ground advance had overtaken plans for its use. However, as the armies in France and now Belgium began to lose momentum an opportunity for their use presented its-self. Eisenhower could easily support Montgomery's plan to enhance an earlier operation (COMET) to a corps level airborne operation, as Bradley was far from keen on airborne forces. He and other main US commanders would have preferred to use the transports in the logistic effort to support their armies. The allocation of an airborne corps to Twenty First Army Group was a way of satisfying the demands of both Montgomery and the Pentagon. However, would there be sufficient combat supplies available to support full execution of the plan? In short, no. Alliance politics prevailed over pure military interest.

Intelligence

Not only were the impression of soldiers at the front shaped by lack of opposition and the speed of advance at the end of August 1944 but even normally reserved staff officers were optimistic that the war's end was near. As early as mid August, SHAEF's Intelligence Summary declared:

> *Two and a half months of bitter fighting, culminating for the Germans in a blood-bath big enough even for their extravagant tastes, have brought the end of the war in Europe within sight, almost within reach.'*

All indicators were that the German collapse was total. Tens of thousands of German soldiers were isolated or almost cut-off, in the fortified ports of France and the Low Countries and in early September 1944, the *Volksarmies* that were later to confront the Allies did not yet exist.

During early stages of planning for Operation COMET, some remarkably accurate intelligence painted a less rosy picture on 7 September 1944:

> '... it is reported that one of the broken panzer divisions has been sent back to the area north of Arnhem to rest and refit; this

German garrisons manning the Channel Ports were cut off by the rapid advance of the Allies. Here civilians are allowed to leave the beleagured port of Dunkirk during a truce. It would remain cut off until the end of the war.

might produce some 50 tanks.'

This was the Resistance passing on details of the arrival of the leading elements of the shattered II SS Panzer Corps (9th and 10th SS Panzer Divisions) from France to refit north of the Rhine. The report continues:

9th SS
Hohenstaufen
Panzer Division

'To-day's photographs together with ground reports from Dutch sources, indicate that the main direction of German movement is NW to SE; not only has 347 Div come down, but many of the SS training units which were near AMSTERDAM are now quartered in the excellent barracks at NIJMEGEN. There seems little doubt that our operational area will contain a fair quota of Germans, and the previous estimate of one division may prove to be not far from the mark ... and [that] *a vulnerable outpost of the Fatherland's frontier has been made into a hedgehog defensive position ...'*

10th SS
Frundsberg
Panzer Division

In the optimism of the time, the presence of a 'broken panzer division' and numerous *ad hoc* units did not seem to count as a significant planning factor, although some junior commanders had reservations about their missions. As recounted by Geoffrey Powell:

'At one battalion briefing, a company commander, on hearing the task allocated to a colleague, had leaned over to him and whispered "That should provide you with either a Victoria Cross or a wooden one".'

This tendency to ignore the enemy, as highlighted by Polish airborne General Sosabowski's outburst 'But the Germans, General, the Germans' became even more marked as planning for MARKET GARDEN got under way. A little more than a week later, the intelligence planning documentation failed to mention most of the enemy positions and movements outlined above and ignored the significance of additional material. Accusations of ignoring intelligence that stood in the way of his plan (cognitive dissonance) have been levelled against Montgomery and 1st Airborne Division in particular. Colonel Michael Hickey provides one explanation:

'Monty was very competitive. He wanted, as a battalion commander, his battalion to win all the trophies available in the Egyptian Command in the 1930s, and they probably did. He competed against other generals, particularly in north-west Europe with General Patton, with whom his relationship was a pretty unstable one. They couldn't make each other out as men,

34

because they were so radically different from each other: Patton the dashing, swashbuckling Southern cavalryman in the American army, Monty the ascetic, non-smoking, non swearing, non-drinking Cromwellian. And the competition grew to a head as the Allies broke out of the Normandy pocket and made their bid to go for the German border in the high summer and early autumn of 1944.'

The MARKET GARDEN Plan - Outline

Montgomery left his meeting with Eisenhower at Brussels on 7 September, with the resources of the Allied Airborne Army at his disposal, believing that he had been promised *'absolute priority'* for logistics. His MARKET GARDEN plan, which he personally detailed down as far as divisional tasks, was delivered to General Miles Dempsey, Commander British Second Army on 10 September. It was a bold plan. The crucial part of which was to be commanded by Lieutenant General 'Boy' Browning, with a corps of 1st British and 82nd and 101st US Airborne Divisions. He explained that, in Operation MARKET, the Airborne Corps were to seize important points (mainly rivers and canals) across Holland on an axis from a

Left to right: General Ritchie XII Corps, Lieutenant General O'Connor VIII Corps, Major General D.A.H. Graham 50th Northumbrian Division, Dempsey and Montgomery, reviewing map.

bridgehead on the Escaut Canal, through Eindhoven, Nijmegen and Arnhem. In the GARDEN part of the operation, an armoured spearhead would drive north across the 'Carpet' of airborne troops, to the Zuyder Zee, almost a hundred miles into enemy territory. From here, having outflanked the West Wall and cut off hundreds of thousands of Germans in western Holland, armoured forces would envelop the Ruhr and prepare to strike towards Berlin. Not only was General Bradley surprised at Montgomery's boldness but he added 'Monty's plan was one of the most imaginative of the war.'

It certainly was a bold plan but the whole concept was predicated on the German defences being only a thin crust and that a properly concentrated and well-supported ground force could pierce it and reach the airborne divisions. Montgomery, as we shall see, successfully broke through the German defences on the Escaut Canal but what had not been envisaged was the escape of 82,000 soldiers of the German Fifteenth Army across the mouth of the Scheldt. Nor had it been anticipated that the shattered divisions from France, the North Sea coast and the 'ageing gentlemen of Germanys last reserves', would be able to form an effective defence.

General Lewis Brereton, commanding the Allied Airborne Army, had to bring two elements together in his plan. Firstly, there were the ground troops, represented by the headquarters of the Airborne Corps under Lieutenant General Browning and, secondly his fellow British and American airmen. The plan he developed gave primacy to the airforces' considerations, which arguably contributed to MARKET GARDEN's overall failure. The first decision was a daylight drop. With inexperienced aircrews and a moonless period, a repeat of the badly dispersed drops that opened D-Day did need to be avoided. In addition, Brereton's aircraft fleet was capable of flying less than half of the Airborne Corps in one lift. This was compounded by a lack of ground crew, which led to USAAF Major General Williams, of IX Troop Carrier Command (TCC), recommending to Brereton that there should be only one lift per day. Thus, the airborne divisions were not going to arrive in a single 'clap of thunder' but over a period of three days. As a consequence, only half of the first lift would be available to seize objectives on 17 September, because vital units had to be retained to defend Drop Zones (DZs) and Landing Zones (LZs) for subsequent lifts. Finally, as

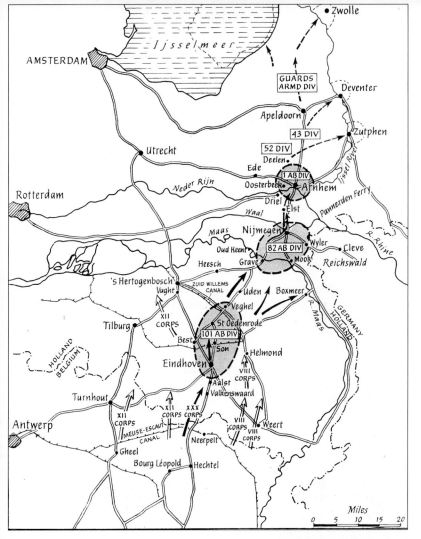

with Normandy the airmen warned of heavy aircraft losses to flak. On this occasion, with the end of the war in sight, there was a general wish to avoid unnecessary casualties and the senior air officers got their way. Consequently, DZs were to be sited away from flak positions and, therefore, also well away from the ground troops' objectives. Crucially, Major General Urquhart had his request for a glider *coup de main* at the Arnhem Bridge turned down. However, even General Gavin (82nd Airborne), arguably MARKET GARDEN's most experienced Allied airborne commander, also lost out to IX TCC's insistence that a *coup de main* on the Nijmegen Bridge was too risky. The air force commander's over-cautious approach to the first lift, based on an understandable desire to avoid casualties, led to considerable losses amongst aircrew over subsequent days.

In advance of the air armada, the Allied airforces were to fly 1,395 bomber and 1,240 fighter or fighter bomber sorties over Southern Holland and the drop zones. In the event, because of these attacks, the transports and gliders were able to carry out the initial drops with minimal losses. The P-51 Mustangs and P-47 Thunderbolts protecting the slow moving columns of

Lieutenant General F. A. M. 'Boy' Browning.

transport aircraft had little to do. On the ground, known troop concentrations in barracks and anti aircraft positions were repeatedly attacked spoiling the Germans' rear combat zone Sunday routine.

General Browning had reservations about MARKET GARDEN, as illustrated by his famous remark to Montgomery 'I think we may be going a bridge too far.' but he was overruled. Having previously offered his resignation over what he saw as Brereton's disregard for ground elements in an earlier operation, he was in no position to influence the plan by repeating his threat. In addition, Major General Urquhart, although he was commanding the most exposed division, lacked airborne experience and, consequently, credibility to convince the airmen to change their plans.

Major-General Roy Urquhart.

101st Airborne Division's Mission and Plan

As was the case with the other airborne divisions, 101st's plan was shaped by the airforces' requirements. Among other stipulations, air planners refused to drop elements of the Division near Eindhoven. They were afraid that transport aircraft would be vulnerable to German flak covering the Phillips electronic factories and the City's airfield. This view precluded a *coup de main* on the Son

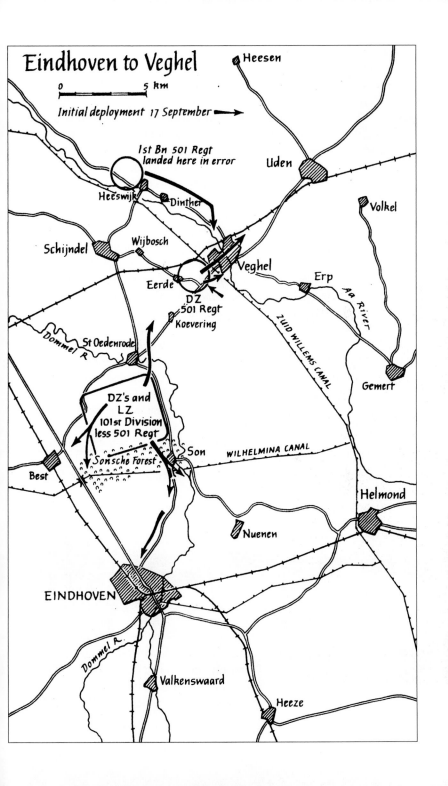

Eindhoven to Veghel

0   5 km

Initial deployment 17 September ➝

Heesen

1st Bn 501 Regt
landed here in error

Uden

Heeswijk   Dinther

Volkel

Schijndel   Wijbosch

Veghel

Erde   Eerde

Erp

Aa River

DZ
501 Regt

ZUID WILLEMS CANAL

Koevering

Dommel R.

St Oedenrode

Gemert

DZ's and
LZ
101st Division
less 501 Regt

Son

WILHELMINA CANAL

Sonsche Forest

Best

Helmond

Nuenen

EINDHOVEN

Dommel R.

Valkenswaard

Heeze

Bridge over the Division's first major waterway. The soldiers also had their considerations. A factor foremost in Major General Maxwell D Taylor's mind was that with MARKET's daylight drop, he was determined that it would be well concentrated. The 'Screaming Eagles' drop by inexperienced aircrews in the early hours of D-Day had been widely dispersed, when evasive action disorientated the crews sufficiently for any form of accuracy to be lost in the dark. The 101st's divisional historian records:

'... So it was arranged to drop both the 502nd and 506th in the area north-west of Son, on Drop Zones B and C respectively, and to use the same area for the later glider landings. Only the 501st was to be dropped separately.

To the 506th, was given the mission of seizing the Wilhemina Canal Bridge at Son, then moving on to the south and taking Eindhoven, with its four highway bridges over the winding Dommel River.

The 502nd was to guard the LZ, to capture the Road Bridge at St Oedenrode, and to be ready to take over the defence of Son and support the 506th in its move south to Eindhoven. General Taylor gave it the additional mission of sending a company to seize the road and railroad bridges at Best, on the flank of the zone of responsibility.

The 501st had the job of capturing the highway and railroad bridges over the Aa River and the Willemsvaart Canal at Veghel. To place it closer to these bridges it was given the separate DZs further to the north.'

Maj-Gen Maxwell D. Taylor, Commander of the US 101st Division 'Screaming Eagles'.

With the Division's first lift allocation of 424 DC-47 Skytrain aircraft (known to the British as the Dakota) and seventy CG-4A Waco gliders, Major General Taylor elected to maximize the infantry he could have immediately available. Accompanying them on Sunday 17 September, were only the slimmest elements of Divisional troops. For instance, no artillery was to be brought in on the first lift, as the leading elements of the British ground troops, accompanied by guns, were due to reach them in Eindhoven by 20.00 hours on the first evening. 101st Airborne Division was allocated the largest number of aircraft for the first lift, on the basis that the operation needed to get off to a good start. The 101st Airborne's fourth infantry regiment 327 Glider Infantry Regiment (GIR) was to be flown in on the second lift on D+2.

Major General Maxwell Taylor described his concept of operations:

> 'The only comparable operation in history that I know of was the defence of the western railroad lines against the Indian raids during the period following our Civil War. We were forced to spread along the highway, garrisoning key towns with the hope of being able to move rapidly to meet hostile thrusts before they could become dangerous. When the enemy was close enough to the road to become dangerous to the traffic on it, he had to be fought and destroyed; on the periphery of this vital zone it was a matter of nice judgement to decide how to discourage the enemy from attacking without becoming involved in a serious engagement.'

XXX Corps Plan

As promised by Lieutenant General Horrocks, the Irish Guards were to lead the Guards Armoured Division and the rest of XXX Corps – borne by over 20,000 vehicles. The Guard's H Hour was co-ordinated with the start of the airborne operation. They were to be blasted through the 'thin' German defences by an artillery barrage and drive forward on a single road to meet the 101st Airborne at Eindhoven. However, at the same time West Countrymen of 231 Infantry Brigade, from 50th Division, were to start expanding the Neerpelt Bridgehead and the Corridor north on foot. No contemporary document laying down exact

information for Operation MARKET GARDEN timings has been found. However, General Horrocks in his divisional orders group, emphasized several times over, 'Speed is absolutely vital, as we must reach the lightly armed 1st British Airborne Division, if possible, **in forty-eight hours**.' The paratroopers holding the northern end of the Arnhem Bridge also expected to be relieved by XXX Corps in two days.

Lieutenant General Horrocks.

With so many major and minor waterways to be crossed, XXX Corps had two Army Groups Royal Engineer assembled on the heaths around Bourg Leopold. 43 Wessex Division who were to follow the Guards were to be prepared to conduct assault and bridging operations if a major bridge was blown.

The Decision to Go

During the days of early June 1944, General Eisenhower had a difficult decision to make. Could he launch the D-Day invasion on Group Captain Stagg's weather predictions or would he have to postpone the invasion. General Louis Brereton had a similar decision to make based on meteorological advice, in mid September: a period of far less stable weather. 21st Army Group's post-operational report for 16 September 1944, recalls

> *'1630 hrs. Lt-Gen BRERETON decided to proceed with Op MARKET. Period 17-20 Sep suitable for airborne ops with fair weather apart from morning fog. Light winds'.*

However, what proved to be variable weather conditions over central and southeast England and Holland were to have a significant impact on the coming battle, which from its conception already had a very slim margin of error.

Lieutenant General Brereton

CHAPTER THREE

BREAKOUT TO VALKENSWAARD
The wait, the ambush and the halt at Valkenswaard

There has been much Post-War development along the road which during the period 10 – 17 September bisected the bridgehead held by the Guards Armoured Division, with the help of the West Countrymen of 231 Brigade. Drive north from Joe's Bridge. Turn left onto the **N74** towards **Eindhoven**. You are now in No Man's Land which lay astride the **Dutch/Belgian border**, two hundred yards beyond the junction.

Sunday 17 September 1944
There was an air of uneasiness in the Neerpelt bridgehead on that Sunday morning in September. The vital foothold remained under command of the Guards Armoured Division but was actually being held by 231 Infantry Brigade detached from 50th Division. At 07.45 hours, a message to XXX Corps read:
'231 Bde report following activities in bridgehead. Enemy has been infiltrating most of the way round. Enemy inf at 368988 one AFV at 372988 and MG at 335981 were all shot up by arty. Regtl shoot was carried out on mortars at 323989. Patrols report enemy in wood at 3500 and on rd at 3700. Furthest enemy penetration was to 367959.'
This was followed at 09.10 hrs by further and more alarming news.
'231 Bde report that they think enemy is reinforcing NORTH of them. Sounds of transport and tps debussing in woods 3501 and 3700. Patrol sent EAST held up at 365959. It appears that enemy are closing in on EAST and WEST and a counter attack is expected at any time.'
With the British drive eastward having been halted for a week the Germans were expecting a renewed offensive from one of the bridgeheads along the Dutch / Belgian frontier.

Waiting for H Hour
It is remarkable that only twenty-four hours after Lieutenant General Horrocks gave his orders, the seemingly interminable series of briefings at the lower levels of command, were

43

PERSONAL MESSAGE FROM THE C-in-C

(TO BE READ TO ALL TROOPS)

1. I want today, 17 September, to speak to all soldiers in the Group of Armies under my command.

2. What a change has come over the scene since I last spoke to you on 21 August. **Then** we were moving up towards the SEINE, having inflicted a decisive defeat on the German armies in Normandy. **Today** the SEINE is far behind us; the Allies have removed the enemy from practically the whole of France and Belgium, except in a few places, and we stand at the door of Germany.

And by the terrific energy of your advance northwards from the Seine, you brought quick relief to our families and loved ones in England — by occupying the launching sites of the flying bombs.

We have advanced a great way in a short time, and we have accomplished much. The total of prisoners captured is now nearly 400,000; and there are many more to be collected from those ports in Britany and in the Pas de Calais that are still holding out.

The enemy has suffered immense losses in men and material; it is becoming problematical how much longer he can continue the struggle.

3. Such a historic march of events can seldom have taken place in history in such a short space of time.

You have every reason to be very proud of what you have done.

Let us say to each other :

« This was the Lord's doing, and it is marvellous in our eyes ».

4. And now the Allies are closing in on Nazi Germany from the east, from the south, and from the west; her satellite powers have thrown the towel into the ring — they have had enough of the Nazis, and they now fight on our side. Our American Allies are fighting on German soil in many places; very soon we shall all be there.

5. The Nazi leaders have ordered the people to defend Germany to the last and to dispute every inch of ground; this is a very natural order, and we would do the same ourselves in a similar situation.

But the mere issuing of orders is quite useless; you require good men and true to carry them out.

The great mass of the German people know that their situation is already hopeless, and they will think more clearly on this subject as we advance deeper into their country; they have little wish to continue the struggle.

6. Whatever orders are issued in Germany, and whatever action is taken on them, no human endeavours can now prevent the complete and utter defeat of the armed forces of Germany; their fate is certain, and their defeat will be absolute.

The triumphant cry now is

« Forward into Germany ».

7. Good luck to you all, and good hunting in Germany.

B. L. Montgomery
Field . Marshal
C-in-C 21 Army Group.

Belgium
17 Sept. 1944.

Personal message from Field Marshal Montgomery.

complete. After three months of campaign, XXX Corps was a highly efficient military organi-zation. With planning and orders complete, at 11.00 hours, General Horrocks moved forward and climbed with his small Tactical (Tac) Headquarters to the roof of the factory south of the Escaut canal. From here, he had an excellent view across the Neerpelt Bridgehead to No Man's Land and the Dutch border beyond. He could clearly see the area of the initial assault; the woods just inside the Netherlands where the German

The road to Valkenswaard. The woods were good concealment for infantry armed with Panzerfausts.

soldiers of 1st and 3rd Battalions of *Fallschirmjäger* Regiment von Hoffmann were dug in. Commander XXX Corps describes the lull before the storm:

'It was a lovely Sunday morning, completely peaceful except for the occasional chatter of a machine-gun in the distance. It was rather a terrible thought that on my word of command "All hell" would be let loose. ... I knew that this would be a tough battle; especially so, owing to the nature of the country, with its numerous water obstacles and the single main road available for thousands of vehicles; but failure never entered my head. While all these thoughts were passing through my head, I was told over the wireless [at 12.30 hours] *that the weather was O.K. and the Airborne Armada was on its way.* [The very British code word 'TALLYHO – Gone away.' was issued by Rear HQ Allied Airborne Corps.] *Even now, I was determined not to give Zero Hour until I actually saw them overhead, as weather conditions could change quickly. I felt a very lonely figure, leaning over the parapet of that factory roof. This was always a difficult time for me, knowing that thousands of men were about to risk their lives in a plan for which I was responsible. I kept on going over the details in my mind. Had I overlooked anything?'*

At 13.10 hours the duty watchkeeper at Main Headquarters XXX Corps and his signallers deciphered a message from General Horrocks' Tac HQ, *'Our Zero Hour is 14.35'*. While the Corps Commander was agonizing from his vantagepoint more junior commanders were assembling their troops and going over final details of their part in the operation.

On the other side of No Man's Land the Germans were awaiting the attack that they were now sure was imminent. Lieutenant Heinz Volz, Adjutant 1st Battalion *Fallschirmjäger* Regiment von Hoffmann, recalls in his regiment's history how;

'At about midday we suddenly discerned an unearthly droning noise coming out of the air. A huge stream of transport aircraft and gliders approached out of the enemy hinterland, flying at an unusually low altitude. This enormous swarm was escorted by countless fighters, in particularly Lightnings. These could observe everything moving on the ground and covered our defensive area in minute detail, engaging anything they could see. Our own anti-air did not react. Only in the hinterland did flak open up.'

The Breakout

At 14.00 hours the waiting was over. Three hundred and fifty guns and heavy mortars opened fire from positions to the south of the bridgehead. Unlike the massive barrages of June and July 1944, the majority of the guns were the relatively light 25-pounders. As a result of logistic/transport difficulties most of

Gun crews of 94th Field Artillery operating 25 pdrs on the heathland south of the Escaut Canal. The area is now a Belgian Army training ground.

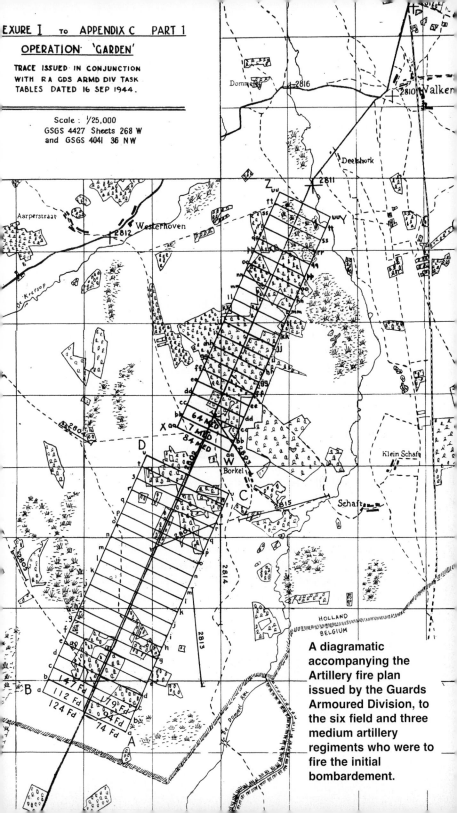

EXURE I to APPENDIX C PART 1

OPERATION 'GARDEN'

TRACE ISSUED IN CONJUNCTION WITH R A GDS ARMD DIV TASK TABLES DATED 16 SEP 1944.

Scale : 1/25,000
GSGS 4427 Sheets 268 W
and GSGS 4041 36 N W

A diagramatic accompanying the Artillery fire plan issued by the Guards Armoured Division, to the six field and three medium artillery regiments who were to fire the initial bombardement.

the medium and heavy guns of the Army Groups Royal Artillery had been left behind, 'grounded' without transport. The target area was almost one-mile wide and extended five miles down the pencil straight road to Valkenswaard. Beyond the artillery targets, the Royal Air Force's medium bombers and no less than eleven squadrons of rocket and cannon firing Typhoons attacked the few identified and numerous likely enemy positions either side of the road. As there were no airphotos available, enemy positions in depth were a matter of guesswork and identification of targets by spotter or attacking aircraft was not easy but eight aircraft from 83 Group attacked the target area every five minutes. Each aircraft made several attacks so that it seemed there was a continuous stream of aircraft roaring in over the treetops at several hundred miles an hour. However, troops that were camouflaged and well dug-in did not make the best fighter-bomber target. Ground attack aircraft were at their most effective when attacking enemy formations moving to a battle area (interdiction) or, as at Falaise, applying the *coup de grâce* to a fleeing mass of humanity. Even so, the RAF caused significant damage to the enemy but more importantly, German morale was undermined. Watching from the Belgian side of the border, the fighter-bombers' display of firepower and the airborne *Armada* certainly impressed XXX Corps.

On the receiving end of the British fire plan were the *Fallschirmjäger* of the Regiment von Hoffman. *Leutnant* Heinz Volz recalls in his regiment's history how;

> 'The front which had been relatively quiet from about midday, suddenly erupted into a hell, as at 14.00 an unearthly crescendo of artillery fire fell on the ring enclosing the bridgehead. For an hour the soil shook time and time again as the defenders were ground down. Captain Brockes was killed by a direct hit from a mortar round on his command post, in a house on the Valkenswaard road. A shell fragment from above penetrated his skull.'

As the thirty-five minute barrage opened, the Irish Guards Group moved up to their Start Line, the infantry riding on the tanks of the second and following squadrons. Typically, General Horrocks had taken the trouble to find out the identity of the men who were to lead the advance, consequently we may with some confidence, picture the events that took place at 2.35pm:

Lieutenant Keith Heathcote, 3rd Squadron, 2nd Battalion Irish Guards, in the turret of his Sherman tank, called into his mike **'Driver advance!'** For Horrocks and his men, the battle for what would become known as 'Hell's Highway' had begun.

The road that the Irish Guards used, now the **N69** to **Valkenswaard** and **Eindhoven**, is raised several feet above the surrounding terrain. German infantry, with their Panzerfausts occupied the woods that the road cuts through, while the more open areas were covered by 88mm guns or 10th SS Panzer Division's assault-guns.

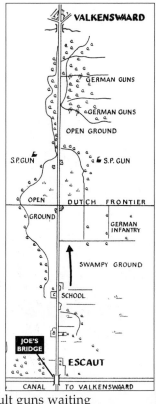

Ambush!

For about ten minutes, all went well. The artillery fire started to roll forward, at a rate of two hundred yards a minute or about seven miles an hour. This rate of advance seemed over optimistic to the experienced Guardsmen. However, it seemed that the Gunners and RAF had successfully neutralized the enemy's outposts along the forward edge of the woods. Certainly, the German towed anti-tank guns, in their relatively exposed positions were all knocked out before they even came into action. However, further back infantry sheltering in their trenches had survived. As the Irish Guards advanced across the Dutch border, the lightly armoured sides of the Shermans made a good target for the *Fallschirmjäger's* hand held anti-tank weapon, the *Panzerfaust*. In true ambush fashion, the Germans let the leading troops through, to be dealt with by the SS assault guns waiting further in depth. The ambush engaged the rear of No. 3 Squadron and the leading tanks of No.1 Squadron, with infantry hanging on to the turret and hull. Nine tanks and two armoured cars were quickly blazing. The Irish Guards regimental historian recounts:

> *'The gunner in Sergeant Capwell's tank put a belt of Browning into a "bazooka boy", and so saved the front half of No. 3 Squadron which like a mutilated lizard, went careering on*

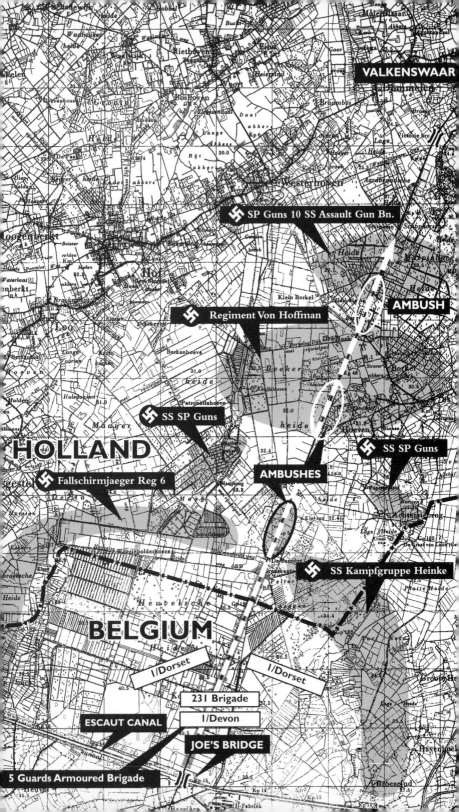

VALKENSWAAR

SP Guns 10 SS Assault Gun Bn.

AMBUSH

Regiment Von Hoffman

SS SP Guns

HOLLAND

SS SP Guns

Fallschirmjaeger Reg 6

AMBUSHES

SS Kampfgruppe Heinke

BELGIUM

I/Dorset

I/Dorset

231 Brigade

I/Devon

ESCAUT CANAL

JOE'S BRIDGE

5 Guards Armoured Brigade

until Major M O'Cock's wireless cries of "Hi! You've lost your tail", brought them to a halt'.

Lieutenant Volz continues his description of the *Fallschirmjäger's* part in the battle:

'A large number of English tanks were soon knocked out by Panzerfausts, firing from five to ten metres away. For the first time, we were able to impose a decisive block, because the terrain to the left and right of the road was not suitable for tanks, being boggy, and probably, also thought to be mined.'

Wounded or simply shocked and dazed, some of the Guards tank crews fell into German hands. However, one guardsman recalls that he was somewhat luckier!

'I bailed out and made for the nearest cover, which was a seemingly empty German slit trench. In I went but I found my-

Leading armoured vehicles charged into German tank ambushes. Here Fallschirmjäger disable a British armoured car.

A dead Irish Guardsman hanging from the turret of his knocked out Sherman tank.

self sharing it with a fat and very frightened Hun, who obligingly moved up as much as he could to let me in! He then offered me a large cigar!'

Others were up against more determined individuals as the Corps history records.

'Another had a sharp scuffle with the German occupant of his trench, and shot him in the stomach. The wounded German fired back, and hit the Guardsman in the leg, but he quickly finished the Hun off.'

Despite stopping the attack, all was not well with the execution of the German's plan. The divisional chief of staff of *Kampfgruppe* Walther explained:

'Instead of selecting the major road to Valkenswaard as the main effort of the defence, it was designated as a boundary between units. Consequently nobody really wanted to feel responsible for the road'.

Matters were further complicated as radio and line communications amongst the *ad hoc* German force failed. As the battle developed the various German unit headquarters moved back as the Allies advanced. This meant that, without knowing the new location of

British tanks pass a knocked out Irish Guards Sherman on Hell's Highway. (Inset) The German *Panzerfaust* – an extremely effective one-shot weapon.

Fallschirmjäger **mortar crew.**

headquarters the Germans could not even resort to runners as an effective method of communication. A situation report from Guards Armoured Division is recorded in XXX Corps battle log:

> *'Leading Sqn IG got through. Remainder held up in area 3799 by 200 inf dug in each side of toll rd and a few SP guns. Have put in a set piece attack, which is now in progress. Typhoons helping. Appears from PW and marked maps that there is not much behind. One Bn 9 SS reported by PW to be at NEERPELT.'*

At the same time, 16.25 hours, a staff officer recorded that,

> *'Coms established with Airborne Corps – messages now being passed – strength 1-2 [on a scale of 1-5].'*

The weak and barely workable link with General Browning's headquarters was a timely reminder that ahead lay almost 30,000 Allied paratroops that XXX Corps had to reach.

There isn't a single point that can be said to be the exact area of the ambush, as the Germans let the Irish Guards deep into their position, before opening fire. The forward German outposts were just beyond the border crossing and extended back along the road for several miles. By holding their fire, the Germans ensured that they were able to attack the maximum number of British tanks. The German infantry made use of the cover offered by the woods alongside the road and the anti tank

A Typhoon I.B, R.A.F., fully armed with rockets, these were called upon to assist the Guards in clearing the Highway.

guns the longer fields of fire across the open ground between the woods.

Firepower to the Rescue

With the advance stalled and tanks burning on the road, with the infantry sheltering in ditches alongside, the Guards resorted to superior weight of firepower to blast their way forward. Travelling with the two Vandeleur cousins, who commanded the infantry and tanks of the Irish Guards Group, were RAF forward air controllers, mounted in an M3 White half-track. Their task was to pass instructions to the waiting 'cab-rank' of 83 Group Typhoons circling overhead. During the next hour the RAF officers called in two hundred and thirty sorties on five miles of road and its immediate surrounding area. To help, the Guards fired red smoke shells to indicate target areas, while worried troop leaders threw yellow smoke grenades to indicate their own position to the pilots approaching at two hundred miles an hour. Clearly, they did not completely trust the fluorescent orange air identification panels positioned on the rear of each vehicle. With smoke and radio orders pinpointing targets the Typhoons' rocket and cannon fire was far more effective than it had been during the preliminary sorties. Also adding to the maelstrom of fire, were the gunners who were now able to engage targets identified by the Guards as they advanced. Once targets had been neutralized, the Guards resumed their advance. The remaining Irish Guards' tanks of the leading squadrons had withdrawn back to the area of the border. Partly to keep a safe distance between them and the fighter-bomber targets and partly, as their historian put it, *'to get a flying start past the shattered hulls of the knocked-out tanks'.* However, the bulldozer taken on transporter in case a crossing of the Dommel was needed, became stuck across the road and caused a frustrating delay. The feelings of the hapless driver and the watching commanders can be readily imagined! General Horrocks describes the RAF pilots as superb,

> *'and the Typhoons literally shot the infantry onto their objectives, the rockets landing within 200 yards of our leading troops. Nothing could stand up to this and after some bitter infantry fighting the enemy crust was pierced'.*

As the dust thrown up by rocket and shell began to subside, a sharp eyed pilot identified and attacked several 88mm guns lying in wait, covering the road in the area of Hoek. However, a Typhoon was also responsible for the destruction of two Shermans, who now moving, could not rely on yellow smoke to identify them. Fratricide, in war is certainly not a new phenomenon.

During the renewed advance, with their infantry dismounted and deployed either side of the road, the advance of the Irish Guards Group continued. A combination of the stunning effect of the second bombardment, HE and machine gun fire from the tanks and the threat of direct attack by the Irish Guard's Number 1 Company, worked its usual magic. Lieutenant Volz's battalion lost heavily in further less successful

A Sherman on Hell's Highway near the Dutch border passing a knocked out German 88.

attempts to ambush the Irish Guards:

> *'It is certain that a large number of German soldiers were killed here, but unfortunately I do not know their names. Many of our comrades later declared missing also probably disappeared here. The fighting was extremely bitter, and a fox hole sheltering a wounded man can easily be collapsed by a waltzing tank.'*

The Irish Guards record that during the afternoon,

> *'The Intelligence spent the day in a state of indignant surprise: one German regiment after another appeared which had no right to be there.'*

However, by 17.05 hours XXX Corps were being informed that 'Things are beginning to loosen up. Quite a number of PW taken.' Amongst the unexpected German units, near Valkenswaard, were SS-*Hauptsturmführer* Roestler's company of Stugs (assault-guns mounted on Mk IV chassis), which had been detached from 10th *Frundsberg* SS Panzer Division. The remaining eight Stug IVs, out of an original strength of fifteen a couple of hours earlier, attempted to form a blocking position, as the Irish Guards approached Valkenswaard. However, their scope for manoeuvre was restricted by the terrain and they soon fell prey to Allied tank fire and Typhoons. XXX Corps history records that:

Infantry of 231 Brigade, probably 2/Devons, following up behind the Guards Armoured Division towards Valkenswaard.

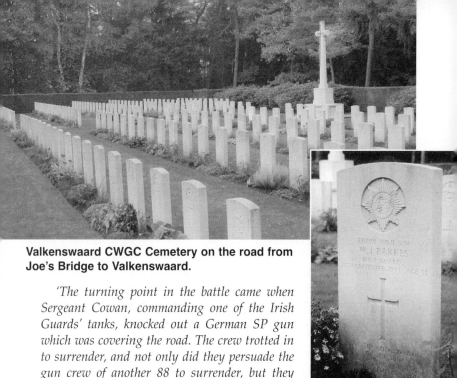

Valkenswaard CWGC Cemetery on the road from Joe's Bridge to Valkenswaard.

'The turning point in the battle came when Sergeant Cowan, commanding one of the Irish Guards' tanks, knocked out a German SP gun which was covering the road. The crew trotted in to surrender, and not only did they persuade the gun crew of another 88 to surrender, but they willingly pointed out the positions occupied by their comrades.'

The grave of Sergeant Major W.J Parkes, Irish Guards, killed on Hell's Highway 1944.

The **Valkenswaard CWGC Cemetery**, where many victims of the fighting on 17 September lie, is on the left just beyond the **Hoek crossroads**. See Appendix III for details.

The Flanks

Orders for their part in the attack only reached the rifle companies of 231 Brigade at 11.00 hours. 2/Devon's and 1/Dorset's tasks were to follow up immediately behind the leading elements of the Irish Guards and to clear the ground for a thousand metres either side of the road. This would involve, with the support of Cromwells from C Squadron 15/19 Hussars, the clearance of identified enemy positions, as well as woods that were likely to conceal enemy anti-tank guns. 2/Devons, who were to lead for the first three miles through the 'Crust', had barely left their Start Line and crossed the Dutch border before the Irish Guards' Shermans were burning on the road to their front. The Devons, their positions clearly marked by orange smoke had a grandstand view of the air attacks and only advanced once the column of tanks was again moving northwards. B and D Companies cleared the woods on the left of the road commanded by the Second in Command, while on the right, the Commanding Officer, set about clearing the larger woods with A and C Companies and tanks of 15/19 Hussars. The Hussar's historian describes their part in the battle:

> 'The main difficulty was for our Troops to keep in touch with the infantry in the thick woods, which confined our tanks to tracks and rides. Sometimes we were behind and sometimes in front of our friends and the support which we gave them was for the most part of moral value only. These troops did, however, fire their Besas [tank machine guns] to help the infantry along when they were sure of their position and when they could see more than a few yards. Captain Swanwick's tank was hit in the engine. Otherwise these Troops did not incur any casualties.'

The going for the Devons and Hussars was also slow on the left flank, where:

> 'there was a halt while the infantry collected some scattered and dazed Germans, who were still cowering in their foxholes. The road was full of tanks moving slowly forward in a solid mass behind the Irish Guards.'

At this stage, it became apparent that, either side of the road the enemy had laid extensive minefields, as 15/19 Hussars lost several vehicles to Teller mines. Casualties included one of C Squadrons Challengers the Cromwell version of the Sherman firefly, mounting a highly effective, 17-pounder gun rather than the normal 75mm. By nightfall, 2/Devons with two troops of

A Challenger version of the Cromwell tank with its 17 pdr gun.

A Carrier and 6-pounder Anti-tank gun crossing the Dutch-Belgian border between Joe's Bridge and Valkenswaard.

Cromwells had reached their objectives at Hoek. Behind 2/Devons, Lieutenant Colonel AEC 'Speedy' Bredin, commanding 1/Dorset, champed at the bit ready to take over the clearance of the road's flanks from Hoek to Valkenswaard, which he was due to take over from the Irish Guards.

Traffic Jams

Within little more than two hours of Zero Hour, traffic jams on Club Route had already appeared. Lieutenant Colonel Bredin, recalls how:

'I ordered the companies (first C Company in T.C.V.s [Troop Carrying Vehicles]) *forward to the road junction just north of the Dutch border, and again went to see the Irish Guards. By now the main road was so congested along its entire length by double and triple banking of tanks and other vehicles that, not only did the battalion vehicles have great difficulty in moving up, but I, Commanding Officer, had to do a bit of pillion-riding on Cpl Barnes' motor-cycle*

The concrete road was almost impossible to mine, however, along the verges, in the area of the front line the Germans had laid mines. As the correspondent Chester Wilmot explained:

'On the first evening two three-toners, following the armour,

had been destroyed by mines which the Germans had laid in the grass verges immediately beside their roadblock. In passing through this, the two trucks had gone off the concrete on to the grass and had been blown up. Next morning the wreckage of these vehicles was seen by all drivers moving north and lest the warning should be disregarded, some over-conscientious Sapper had set up a notice: "DON'T LET THIS HAPPEN TO YOU. KEEP ON THE ROAD. VERGES NOT CLEARED OF MINES".'

Consequently, drivers had a level of mine awareness that contributed to the traffic jams, as they understandably feared to pull off the road onto the verges. Chester Wilmot tried to travel back down the route the following day:

'On the afternoon of the 18th, returning to file a dispatch, I found a traffic jam, two vehicles wide, almost the whole way from the Valkenswaard bridge to the Meuse - Escaut Canal. I was able to move south only by driving along the verge of the road.'

Clearly, Wilmot's assessment that the Germans were unlikely to mine what had been their own lines of communication was correct.

For the majority of the men of XXX Corps, their abiding memory of Operation GARDEN was of their vehicles slowly crawling forward and the never ending, unexplained, halts. Then to be called forward, past other units who had been relegated in priority, only to be halted again. In the subsequent days, it took 43rd Wessex Division almost three days to transit the sixty miles to the frontline. This move forward was hardly likely to promote a sustained sense of urgency amongst the uncomfortable and fitfully slumbering troops of XXX Corps. American paratroops were to complain that a group of Allied Airborne Army staff officers sat lumpenly in their car as a battle was fought out around them!

On the afternoon of 17 September, north of Hoek, another threat to the road was posed by the remaining assault-guns of SS-*Hauptsturmführer* Roestel's command. These vehicles, now using the close cover of the woods, unlike the ground mounted 88 mm guns, did not fall easy prey to the advancing British tanks. They were able to advance on the road, engage and then withdraw. While not stopping the advance, they remained in action and contributed to the delays but their

Vehicles of the Irish Guards Group and 1 Dorset in the church square at Valkenswaard, on the morning of 18 September. Now the square is normally full of parked cars rather than tanks and trucks.

presence was to have a significant impact on a decision made as darkness set in.

Continue along the road towards **Valkenswaard**. Just before reaching the town, the road bends to the right. Here the road crosses the little stream of the River Dommel. The original bridge was very narrow and was causing a problem for two-way traffic on the morning of 18 September and a Bailey bridge was built alongside to eliminate this 'choke-point'.

Valkenswaard – Sunday 17 September 1944

'Sunset is at 18.47 and last light at 19.41 hours'

Finally, at 17.30 hours, the Irish Guards were through both the Germans' prepared and improvised positions, reaching the bridge over the River Dommel, just south of Valkenswaard. The bridge was intact, so after all the frustration and annoyance, the armoured bulldozer, brought up with the leading tanks to improvise a crossing, was not needed. The Historian of the Irish Guards gives a wry account of the Group's entry to

Valkenswaard:

*'The report that the bridge though only a temporary
structure, was intact and fit to carry tanks was welcome, as no
one was looking forward to spending part of the night in the
woods with the bazooka boys. ... No.3 Squadron were more
warlike and took four 88-mms from their unnerved German
crews. Lieutenant B.C. Isitt, thinking it rash to leave such
dangerous things as 88s lying about, tried to destroy them, but
only succeeded in firing into the middle of the Group H.Q. The
German infantry in the woods round the bridge were not as
pusillanimous as the 88-mm crews. Their snipers were
particularly active, one of them wounding Lieutenant Cyril
Russell. Colonel Vandeleur had bursts of Spandau machine-gun
fire just beside him, but no Germans came so near the mark as
Lieutenant Isitt.*

*'The reshuffle of groups and the crossing of the bridge took a
considerable time. No. 2 Squadron and No. 4 Company
approached Valkenswaard very cautiously, while a battery put
concentrations* [of artillery fire] *down on likely points of
resistance. It was already dark; the only light came from houses
set on fire by shelling. We finally battered our way into the place
expecting to find it a complete shambles. Well it more or less
was, with three or four really big fires burning, the streets
strewn with debris, some Germans still firing, and other
Germans milling about trying to find their way back to
Germany. Yet all the inhabitants stood around in the streets
yelling themselves hoarse and getting in the way of the fighting.'*

The Irish Guards Group established its headquarters at the
recently vacated German Headquarters in the Post Office
building in the Town Square. At 21.40 hours, Guards Armoured
Division was confirming to XXX Corps that 'IG Group is in
centre of VALKENSWAARD and has blocked all approaches.'
Shortly after the Guard's arrival, the Town Clerk, having
formally greeted them, took a telephone message for the now
departed German garrison. He took great delight in passing the
message to Colonel Joe that read, 'they [the Germans] were to
hold on at all costs and that reinforcements were on their way'.
This message was a serious incentive to break free of the excited
crowds and deploy to positions on the northern edge of the
town. However, the expected-counter attack did not materialize
until the following morning.

Continue into the town. The centre of **Valkenswaard** is relatively unchanged. Where tanks crammed into the square in 1944 there is now plenty of car parking, with a selection of bars and restaurants opposite.

The Overnight Halt

During the course of the afternoon, Lieutenant Colonels Bredin (CO 1/Dorset) and Vandeleur agreed between them that they could continue the advance to link up with the Americans at Eindhoven, only five miles further north. However, once the Irish Guards Group had reached Valkenswaard, they were ordered to stay in the town until dawn. Much critical debate on the MARKET GARDEN Campaign has centred on this overnight halt. Most judgements have been made with the benefit of hindsight and many have been entirely superficial views. These are the facts.

Firstly, British tactical doctrine for armoured forces was that they did not fight at night. With limited vision and the noise of tracks and engine denying the use of that all important night sense, hearing, this is understandable.

Secondly, XXX Corps had been ordered not to move at night, as lights would have been necessary and, on a single road with open flanks, vehicles would have been extremely vulnerable. With the ending of 'double daylight saving time', night fell early and the delays imposed on the Irish Guards breakout, meant that Eindhoven could not be reached. In hindsight, an H Hour that was well after mid-day, was far too late for XXX Corps. It guaranteed that they would only reach their nearest objectives.

Thirdly, the Irish Guards had fought a significant battle and lost ten tanks or a fifth of their strength. While the remaining tanks had plenty of fuel, their ammunition was depleted and no commander is prepared to set off on an advance deep into enemy territory already low on ammunition. The Irish Guard's Echelon vehicles were caught in the traffic jams and, consequently, no resupply was immediately available.

Fourthly, there was no indication that the vital Son Bridge had been blown. A message that cascaded down the chain of command from Second Army's RAF liaison officer,

'Tactical Air Recce reports, 1530 hrs ... Brs intact ... E443225 rd br at Son ...'

This recce aircraft must have flown over the bridge just before, as we will see shortly, it was blown when the Americans

63

approached. If word that the bridge was blown had reached XXX Corps during early evening on 17 September, it would certainly have made a significant difference to the Guards Armoured Division's plan for the night. Finally, to their rear the enemy between Hoek and Valkenswaard were far from beaten and posed a significant threat. 2/Devons were closing in on Hoek, having had a difficult time clearing the flanks northwards from the border. With only patrols between Hoek and the Irish Guards, there was a very real chance that the corridor would be cut behind them.

Late in the evening, disturbing news did, however, reach the Guards via 2/HCR and the telephone to Son 244. They spoke to an American major, who informed them that the Son Bridge, north of Eindhoven, had been blown. This very bad news meant that the Guards would have to bring forward a bridging task group of men, vehicles and equipment from the Engineer Park situated well behind the Escaut Canal. The traffic jams on the road would have to be cleared and assembling the troops and pressing on in the darkness before dawn, without the Royal Engineers, was pointless.

It has also recently emerged that Brigadier Sir Alexander Stanier (Commander 213 Brigade) ordered 1/Dorset not to advance to Valkenswaard and release the Irish Guards to continue to Eindhoven. 1/Dorset's Main Headquarters, some time before 20.00 hours, received a message and it made the fiery Lieutenant Colonel 'Speedy' Bredin far from happy.

> 'The need for speed was impressed on us and having broken through we were halting for no good reason. Giles [Vandeleur] was justifiably furious.'

At 21.00 hours, 1/Dorset's brand new Adjutant, Captain WB Storey, summarized the situation in the Battalion war diary:

> 'Bn HQ and S Coy arrive and are dispersed up track 3730012 [2 kms north of the border]. It is now raining and pitch-dark, the enemy is all around us, and mortaring commences along line of rd, but 300 yds east of it.'

At 23.30 hours, a liaison officer from Brigade Headquarters delivered a personal note from the Brigadier to the Commanding Officer explaining the situation:

> 'My dear Bredin
> My LO will explain what I want. First of all, you have done well to get in the position you are in & I hope you are not

annoyed in the night by the enemy. I understand you have 90 Fd Regt in your midst. The Irish Gds are calling for you to go & take over Valkenswaard. But I do not think you can do this in the middle of the night.

What I want you to do, is to protect 90 Fd Regt tonight & push on at the earliest possible moment in the morning with part of the Bn (at first light) & take over Valkenswaard, whilst the remainder of the Bn, say two coy groups mops up the woods on either side of the road between Hoek & Valkenswaard. ...'

Clearly, Brigadier Stanier was concerned about protection of his artillery, which had deployed off the road, on an open flank and by the fact that the area between 2/Devons' forward positions at Hoek and Valkenswaard had not been cleared. Infantry advancing on foot or by vehicle at night would have been extremely vulnerable to ambush and 2/Devons, had already suffered the heaviest casualties of the first day of MARKET GARDEN in reaching Hoek. The situation was eventually confirmed by HQ Guards Armoured Division who had no choice but to tell Colonels Joe and

JOE Vandeleur following his promotion to Brigadier shortly after MARKET GARDEN.

Giles Vandeleur to remain in Valkenswaard over night. In short, blame cannot be laid at the feet of the Irish Guards for the halt on the night of 17 September. The fault lies squarely with the MARKET GARDEN H Hour (determined by air requirements) and the Operation's over optimistic planning assumptions. Despite the events of the afternoon, XXX Corps's confidence in success had not been shaken. Guardsman Fitzgerald recalled:

'We had been hit hard but we got through and we expected that, with the airborne in front of us this would be another Monty victory. We were used to hard fighting but we were sure we would succeed'.

Monday 18 September 1944

After an uncomfortable, cold and wet night, Colonel Bredin's Battalion HQ and two companies of 1/Dorsets set out, at 04.30 hours, to Valkenswaard. A Company were mounted on the Cromwells of 15/19 Hussars, with C Company following in trucks. By 06.30 hours they had taken over defence of the town from the 'Micks' and were developing it into a strong point. By 07.10 hours, 1/Dorsets were summoning B and D Companies forward but fighting their way forward through renewed traffic jams meant that the relief of the Irish Guards was not complete until 09.00 hours. Having put the town into a state of defence, the Dorsets sent out patrols to find the enemy and to give warning of the approach of attackers. During this period full and highly profitable co-operation with the Dutch Resistance (PAN) was developed that contributed to the flow of information back to XXX Corps. The Dorsets were to hold Valkenswaard for several days until its importance was negated by the slow, resource starved, flanking advance of VIII and XII Corps.

Lieutenant Colonel 'Speedy' Bredin, CO 1 Dorset, is briefed by members of the Dutch underground in Valkenswaard during 18 September 1944.

CHAPTER FOUR

THE ADVANCE TO EINDHOVEN AND THE SON BRIDGE

The Guards' advance continues and the
liberation of Eindhoven

German communication intercept at 04.15 hours on 18
September 1944, read:

'There is no doubt about it the enemy has broken through'
Telephone log LXXXVIII Korps.

Following the previous afternoon's battle, Headquarters 1st
Fallschirmjäger Army was reeling from the chaos caused by the
Allied attack. A staff officer recalls:

*'There was a feeling of helplessness, an inability to cope in the
face of such an overwhelming blow. Fallschirmjäger Regiment 6
withdrew on its own initiative, moving westward until it made
contact with 85th Infantry Division.'*

General Chill's 85th Division was holding the western side of
the narrow salient or 'Corridor'. To the east, Headquarters of
Kampfgruppe Walther were attempting to bring order to a battle
that had been similarly shaped by the Allied armour's advance.

Guards Armoured Division – Monday 18 September 1944

Follow the **N69** north from Valkenswaard towards **Eindhoven**, through
thickly wooded country to the outskirts of what is now the Eindhoven
suburb of **Aalst**. The crossing of the Tongelreep, where the Germans
blocked the Guards, is now crossed by a main road just before a major
junction and the motorway.

The divisional plan was for the Irish Guards to press on
through Eindhoven to Son and the site of the blown bridge
across the Wilhelmina Canal. Following them was a Royal
Engineer bridging train. *En route* they would link up with the
American's of 101st Airborne Division, who would resume their
advance from Son and capture Eindhoven. Neither the
Americans nor the Guards were entirely sure how much
progress the other had made the previous afternoon. A

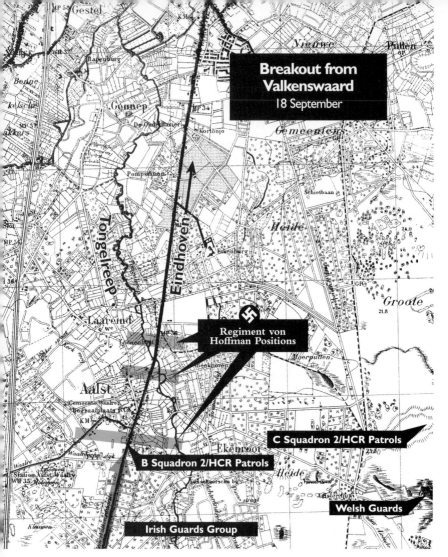

Breakout from
Valkenswaard
18 September

Regiment von
Hoffman Positions

C Squadron 2/HCR Patrols

B Squadron 2/HCR Patrols

Irish Guards Group

Welsh Guards

secondary aim was to expand the breakthrough with the Welsh
Guards, who were to fan out to the north-east, in order to
develop alternative routes and protect the main axis of advance.

Spearheading the secondary advance to the north-east, were
the armoured cars of C Squadron 2/HCR. They had spent an
uncomfortable night halted south of Valkenswaard:

'... *sleeping by the side of the road, with a long line of vehicles
double banked back into Belgium. "Thank goodness," wrote a
trooper "there was little enemy shelling and no enemy planes".*'

Major Herbert's Squadron did its best to fan out to the east of

68

the town but they were halted after only three miles, as they approached the village of Leende. On the road though the wooded country, a combination of the remaining *Sturmgeschütz* belonging to SS-*Hauptsturmführer* Roestel's *Kampfgruppe* and infantry *Panzerfaust* ambushes checked the advance. Fruitless attempts to find an alternative route occupied C Squadron 2/HCR and the Welsh Guards with their Cromwell tanks, for most of the morning. With an alternative route to the east of

Tonglreep Bridge

The original road into Aalst is now a major Eindhoven highway.

Valkenswaard blocked, minor roads outflanking the enemy were sought. However, the bridges over the numerous small waterways were weak and, barely taking an armoured car, they collapsed when crossed by a Cromwell tank. Eventually the frustrated Welsh Guards Group were called back to the 'Centre Line' The 'expanding torrent' of the Allied *Blitzkrieg* had failed as a result of the ground and a low tempo of operations. Lack of progress to the east meant that the Corridor was denied vital width to absorb enemy attacks and, consequently, it remained extremely vulnerable.

On the 'centre line' north, B Squadron 2/HCR's advance was delayed by poor visibility until it was 'likely that they would see the enemy without actually colliding with him!' At 05.30 hours, Lieutenant Tabour's Troop led the advance, a mile and a half ahead of the remainder of the Squadron. If, as was confidently expected, he found the road blocked the following troops would fan out to the east and west to find alternative routes. 2/HCR's historian records that:

'*Corporal Sparrow was in command of the leading scout car. The road out of Valkenswaard ran for several miles through dense pinewoods, opening out at a later stage into flat, sandy country. It was misty and visibility was down to 400 yards when, after advancing approximately two miles, Sparrow suddenly sighted a Panther tank and two self-propelled guns in a side turning. The crew of the Panther were sitting on top of their tank and he gave them a long burst from his Bren gun before retiring out of sight. Lieutenant Tabour, on reporting this opposition was ordered to remain in observation pending the arrival of the tanks of the Irish Guards. However, the infantry arrived first and the position was explained to them. Before anything could be done about it, however, there was a rumbling sound and all three German vehicles drove out of the side turning and were off up the road towards Aalst. The two scout cars were after them like terriers, and after another mile or so one of the self-propelled guns was sighted on the outskirts of Aalst.'*

Meanwhile, Major Wignal, officer commanding B Squadron 2/HCR, ordered his reserve troops to deploy and find alternative routes north, in the immediate vicinity of Aalst.

Major Kerutt, the senior surviving officer of Regiment von Hoffman, had deployed the remnants of his 1st and 3rd Battalions, a platoon of 20mm quad anti-aircraft guns and eleven highly effective 75mm anti-tank guns along the southern edge of Aalst. To add depth, to his position, elements of this force were deployed beyond the Tongelreep stream, about a mile to the rear. By 10.20 hours, Major Kerutt was reporting to 85th Division 'contact with enemy armour in front of Aalst'. Two hours later, he was reporting that he was 'under attack by tanks'. The two-hour delay following the first contact was due to the difficulty in getting the Irish Guards Shermans to the front of the column, as the infantry had been leading through the woods between Valkenswaard and Aalst. Supported by heavy artillery fire, from two entire regiments of 25-pounders, the Irish Guards were able to approach Aalst. The leading tank, a Sherman Firefly of Number 2 Squadron, commanded by Lance-Sergeant Cowan spotted an enemy self-propelled gun.

'I engaged it with five rounds, scoring several targets [hits] but there was no reaction and the "Stable Boy's" armoured cars continued on into the village.'

The Irish Guards Group swept on into Aalst; the infantry fanning out to protect the tanks, with the enemy having seemingly melted away.

However, the advance came to an abrupt halt after little more than a kilometre, as the next water obstacle to the north of the village was guarded by an assault-gun and anti-tank guns. As true recce soldiers, Lieutenant Tabour dismounted three men from his armoured cars and, with him, they stealthily moved forward on foot for a closer look at the enemy positions. While they were observing, a German motor bike and sidecar pulled up alongside the gun. Lieutenant Tabour succumbed to the temptation to engage the target:

> 'We gave it a good long burst of Bren, which must have annoyed the S.P. gun as it fired three rounds of armour-piercing shot at us in quick succession'.

Shortly afterwards, the assault-gun withdrew and Lieutenant Tabour and Lance Corporal of Horse Sparrow, returning to their cars, followed it into a carefully baited ambush.

> 'Rather naturally, their weather eye was on the right of the road, which was the way taken by the S.P. gun, and it was therefore a nasty surprise when two 88-mm guns [probably 75mm] in emplacements opened fire from the opposite side at a range of no more than 200 yards. Sparrow put down smoke and reversed, but Tabour could not do the same for fear of blinding Sparrow's driver, Trooper Price. He therefore opened fire with his Bren to distract the enemy gunners. Both armoured car crews got back to cover without being hit, although the anti-tank guns fired seven rounds at the retiring scout cars in rapid succession'

The Irish Guard's tank commanders, who had closed up to the bridge, were, unsurprisingly, according to Lieutenant Tabour 'grateful that the planned German ambush had been foiled'.

Initially No 2 Squadron and No 2 Company thought that with dash they could repeat the Regiment's success at Joe's Bridge but they lacked that all-important element of surprise.

Sturmgeschütz (StuG) 75mm assault gun/tank destroyer covered with foliage to camouflage it against Allied air attack.

Bursts of enemy machine gun fire and anti-tank rounds convinced them that Major Kerutt's *Kampfgruppen* and the SS assault-guns were a different quality of enemy from that encountered so far. Colonel Joe arriving at the front, immediately assessed the situation and called for an air strike by Typhoons and received the answer that 'No Typhoons available yet today.' Autumnal mist and fog had closed the Allied airfields in southern England and in France. The German anti-tank guns, in prepared concrete positions, blocked the Allied advance on the main axis. The spearhead of XXX Corps was forced to content itself with engaging the enemy with artillery, while an alternative route around the German position was found. This delay south of Eindhoven, was in an area that should have been cleared by 101st Airborne, on 17 September. The delay was exacerbated by the lack of tactical air support.

Facing the enemy position on the route north into Eindhoven, Lieutenant Tabour was still in action.

> '*We were successful in finding the top window of a near-by house and ran out a remote* [radio handset] *to it. Our O.P. gave us limited observation over the area occupied by the 88-mm. Guns ... Once installed, we called for artillery fire and were given good support. We had several shoots at the 88-mms, and as a result of another shoot there was a large explosion that I believe to have been an S.P. gun destroyed by a direct hit.*'

Contributing significantly to the British artillery battle was a manager from the Philips factory in the city, who had over the preceding days the opportunity to observe the German defensive preparations, as he cycled to and from work. He provided a precise sketch map that enabled the Guard's artillery to pinpoint the enemy positions. Subsequent examination of wrecked German equipment in the areas engaged, proved that the Dutchman's information had been extremely accurate.

The Grenadier Guards Group Flanking Movements – Monday 18 September 1944

It will be recalled that, at the initial contact with the enemy, C Squadron 2/HCR had fanned out eastwards under cover of early morning mist and that enemy action and impassable water obstacles precluded an advance on this flank. However, to the west, the Grenadier Guards had started to make slow progress around Eindhoven. Lieutenant Palmer's troop made

An abandoned German 88mm anti-aircraft gun. A weapon with a formidable reputation amongst the Allies, especially when employed in the anti-tank role against Shermans and Churchills

their way across a maze of,

> '*small streams spanned by fragile wooden bridges, until, they eventually found a way across the River de Run, and thereafter the route improved.*'

The few Germans they encountered were surprised that even light armoured cars would be attempting to take such a precarious cross-country route. Travelling with the HCR was an American sergeant with a radio who continuously attempted to contact Headquarters 101st Airborne Division to warn them of the problems and the alternative route they were taking.

The Grenadier's advance was not, however, straightforward. Lieutenant Palmer recalls:

> '*My Troop led the Squadron down a narrow road across some very open flat country. I came to a dyke some 20 feet across with*

banks about 6 feet deep with what appeared to be plenty of water in it. The bridge, of wooden construction, looked very weak, so I stopped my tank short of it, got out and had a look. The bridge did not appear likely to take the weight of my tank. I remounted and reported this to the squadron leader [by radio]. *He was of course some way back, not at the site, and also a most forceful and brilliant leader. I was told fairly abruptly that the cavalry had reported it suitable for tanks, and so would I please get on with it! I therefore told my driver to take the bridge as fast as he could in order to get to the other side. This could have been a mistake, for if we had crept over it we might have set up less vibration. As we reached the centre, I felt the bridge subside a bit, but we got over without it collapsing. However, as I looked back I saw a gap at each end about a foot wide and also that the bridge was sagging badly in the middle. My troop sergeant was following some 50 yards back, and I told him over the radio not to attempt it. But by then he was just about on it. On reaching the centre, the bridge finally broke and his tank subsided into the water, on its side and half submerged. Luckily all the crew escaped.'*

In the rapid advance eastwards from Normandy and the demands of subduing the fortified Channel ports meant that armoured bridge layers from 79th Armoured Division *(Hobart's Funnies)* had not been deployed with XXX Corps. In such difficult country, bisected by numerous small waterways, they would certainly have helped with armoured mobility off main routes.

The Liberation of Eindhoven – Monday 18 September 1944

The suburbs of modern Eindhoven have expanded to cover much of the country that 506th Parachute Infantry Regiment fought over to reach the centre of the City in September 1944. Closer in, very little of the original northern suburbs remain and, consequently, it is recommended that the visitor only visits the CWGC Cemetery (see Appendix III) and the Liberation Memorial on **Airbornelaan**. Continue on the **N69** from Valkenswaard, crossing under the **A2 / A67** motorway bridge following signs to **Nijmegen**. Should visitors wish to go to the centre of Eindhoven, look out for the 'Centrum' signs. Otherwise, follow the **Ring Road** to the right (east) and keep following the **Nijmegen** signs around the city. A side trip to the German cemetery at IJsselstijn starts from the Ring Road (see Appendix III). On the northern side of the city, follow signs for **Nijmegen** and **Son**, initially, onto the dual carriageway **N58 (John F Kennedylaan)**. The Eindhoven Liberation Memorial is in a park at the top of the ramp leading to **Airbornelaan**. Parking is difficult, especially at peak travel times. Having visited the memorial return to the **N58** and very shortly turn off the **N58 /** Kennedylaan following signs to **Son en Breughel** on the **N265**.

Seizure of Eindhoven and its four bridges in the city centre over a canal and the River Dommel was one of 101st Airborne Division's objectives for Sunday 17 September. However, with

the blowing of the Son Bridge, Colonel Sink's 506th Parachute Infantry Regiment (PIR) were delayed in crossing the canal, with leading elements stopping for the night in Bokt, north of the city.

Colonel Sink's words, at dawn on Monday 18 September stressed the importance of taking the city.

'If you see any German just let them filter on through you and I guess the "Ducks" [502 PIR's nickname] will take care of them. We have got to get to Eindhoven this morning, and we can't waste any time killing Germans.'

Colonel Sink.

The enemy occupying Eindhoven were largely rear echelon troops, along with disorganized and defeated soldiers pushed back by the Guards the previous afternoon. The delay at the Son Bridge, gave the Germans time to put together a rudimentary defence that was capable of preventing the paratroopers clearing Eindhoven for the passage of the Guards Armoured Division through the city before mid-day. Colonel Sink's plan was to advance down the road from Son and Bokt with two companies of 3/506 PIR. 2/506 and 1/506 PIR followed behind, leaving a small garrison at the Son Bridge, along with engineers who were busy preparing a site for the bridge to be built by their British counterparts. The regimental historian records the start of the operation:

'The hour was 07.30 when 3rd Battalion crossed the LD at Bokt with H and I Companies astride the road and G and HQ going straight down the road. The country was flat and even and the two companies covering the regimental front were able to

cross the fields and ditches at almost a marching pace. ... Only 600 yards beyond the LD, 3rd Battalion encountered rifle and machine gun fire, and from that point all the way to Eindhoven, the column was opposed by little groups of infantry and occasional artillery fire, though the character of the resistance was so weak and irresolute that it had hardly more than a nuisance and delaying effect.'

However, casualties mounted. second Lieutenant David Forney wrote:

'My military career was cut short ... I was hit with some kind of shell and I never went back to duty.'

He was lucky to survive but other officers, moving into positions to observe the enemy, were not so lucky Lieutenant Santasiero recalls that:

'Capt Kiley came up to me looking like an officer – bars, map case and binos in full view. I said "God damm, Kiley! What in the hell are you doing up here? You shine like a f****** officer. You know the Krauts are waiting to kill officers." A sniper killed Kiley.'

Lieutenant Brewer of 1st Platoon, Company E, 2/506 PIR, was over six-foot tall and, with both his map-case suspended casually from his belt and his binoculars hanging around his neck, he also looked every bit an officer. However, he was luckier than Captain Kiley. When a shot hit him he crumpled to the ground 'like a tree felled by an expert lumberman'. Lying wounded, Brewer recalls how he heard a passing paratrooper say, 'Aw, hell, forget him. He's gone, he's gona die'. But he did not die and survived to rejoin his platoon; no doubt to the embarrassment of the paratroopers who had left him for dead.

During the running battle in the outskirts of Eindhoven, the most important targets for the Americans were the enemy's 88mm guns. Sergeant Jack MacLean, following Company I ran into a group of 88s on the road.

'We heard the order "Bazookas up front" and joined an H Company platoon making a flanking move. We ran into a couple of machine gun emplacements and a couple of riflemen. The platoon drove them off and we were able to catch one 88 being backed into an alley. We put three rounds into it, destroying it and killing the crew'.

3/506 PIR continued their advance along the road into the northern suburbs of Eindhoven but came to a halt facing an

German resistance began to stiffen as the Allies approached the borders of the Third Reich. Here a Fallschirmjäger sniper takes aim.

enemy position centred on two 88mm guns, supported by infantry. Colonel Sink came forward and decided that a direct attack would cost him unnecessary casualties and slow the attack. Manoeuvre was required. Giving quick verbal orders to Lieutenant Colonel Strayer, Colonel Sink directed that 3/506 PIR were to fix the enemy in position by maintaining pressure on them from the front but not by attacking. At the same time, 2/506 PIR were to swing left and strike towards the city centre and the four bridges, while Company F was to attack the enemy blocking position from the flank.

With the help of the Dutch Resistance and ordinary members of the public, 2/506 PIR's leading companies, D and E, closed in to finish off the Germans in Eindhoven. The American paratroopers chased, rather than fought the Germans, through the streets, taking prisoners as they went, trusting many of them to the honourable Dutch people, as they pushed on to their objectives. Meanwhile, facing the two 88mm guns, Company F moved to the flank and rear of the enemy positions, guided by Dutch civilians who gave warnings of the approach of enemy soldiers and directions through the streets to guns. Platoon radio operator Joe Hogenmiller described how Company F closed in on the guns:

506th Parachute Infantry in Eindhoven 18 September. The German defenders consisted mainly of Luftwaffe and rear echelon troops.

> *'Lt Hall called his rifle grenadiers and tommy-gunners to get forward to the head of the column. At the corner, a Dutchman stopped them and explained in English that the gun lay just around the corner. Lt Hall immediately sent his men to attack. The block between us and the gun was triangular in shape with Dutch homes on three sides. 2nd Squad, under Sgt Jacobs, took the left side of the block on Woenselschestraat. The 3rd squad with Sgt Griffin, was in reserve position in the centre of the block and the mortar was set up a little forward. Platoon Headquarters and I went with 1st Squad which was to move to the left and to deploy between the houses of Kloosterdreef. Both assault squads took off through the backyard and moved cautiously to the front of the houses. Not a shot was fired – the enemy seemed to have no idea of our presence.'*

The attack from the rear was over quickly, with the highly trained paratroopers taking forty-one surprised Germans prisoner and killing another thirteen. The cost to the Americans was two soldiers wounded. This is an example of how an enemy can be overcome using manoeuvre to create surprise, rather than suffering heavy casualties in a direct attack.

In the city centre, the German 18 Flak Brigade was reporting to LXXXVIII Korps by telephone:

> *'Enemy has penetrated into the north of Eindhoven. Street*

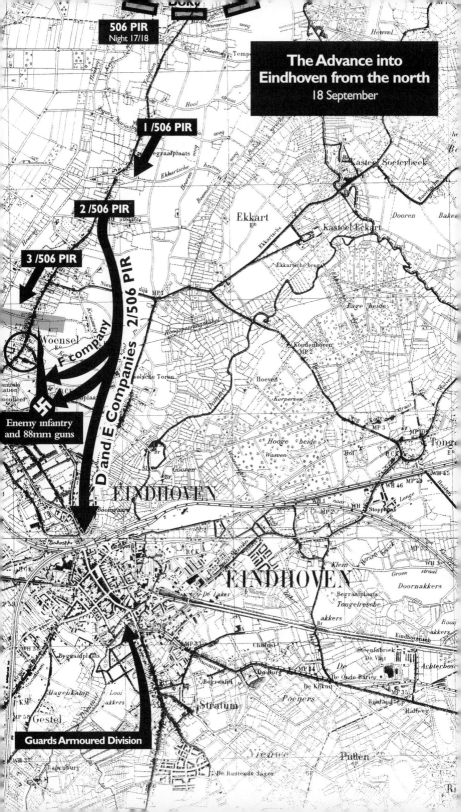

The Advance into Eindhoven from the north
18 September

506 PIR
Night 17/18

1 /506 PIR

2 /506 PIR

3 /506 PIR

D and E Companies 2/506 PIR

F company

Enemy infantry
and 88mm guns

EINDHOVEN

EINDHOVEN

Guards Armoured Division

fighting. Further contact with units not now possible; the insertion of infantry reinforcements has been ruled out. Anti-tank group "Grünewald" requests further orders.'

At which point, the connection was finally cut. As it became clear to the citizens of Eindhoven that the Americans were in the city in greater numbers than the demoralized Germans, the celebrations began. Fine Dutch fruit and schnapps were exchanged for American cigarettes and, to the delight of the children, chocolate! Lieutenant Roy Harmes recalls that, 'Compared with the dour French, the Dutch people's exuberance knew no bounds.' Meanwhile, outflanked, by the Guards, and with the Americans in the city to their rear, German resistance on the southern edge of Eindhoven collapsed. At 12.30, led by C Squadron 2/HCR, the Guards drove on into the city. Lieutenant Tabour describes the scene:

'After all this delay we were most impatient now and now

Below and right: XXX Corps receiving a warm welcome from Dutch civillians as they enter Eindhoven on 18 September.

really had the bit between our teeth. Casting caution to the winds, we moved up the main road at top speed, through Eindhoven and out the other side before the Dutch realized what was happening. Within an hour, we had reached the blown bridge at Son, where we had to remain and settle down for the night.'

Following the HCR was Lieutenant Colonel Joe Vandeleur, who had given the order 'All aboard and motor on!' However, by the time the Irish Guards reached the centre of Eindhoven, they had to force their way through the cheering crowds that blocked the streets. The Allies had liberated their first Dutch city.

Reaching the Son Bridge

The radio report, in lightly 'veiled speech', that the 'Stableboys have contacted our feathered friends' sped up the chain of command. The first of the three link-ups with the airborne divisions had been made. On his arrival, Lieutenant Palmer met Brigadier General Higgins, Assistant Divisional Commander of the Screaming Eagles, who briefed him on the situation and fleshed out the details that had been passed over the civilian telephone about the blown Son Bridge. Royal Engineers advancing with the Guards were now able to speak with the US Airborne engineers, who were already busy preparing approaches to the bridge site. Clearly, there would be a considerable delay while 14 Field Squadron's bridging trains reached the Wilhemina Canal and the Sappers completed work to replace the blown bridge. Arriving a little later, having driven through the crowds in the city, Lieutenant Colonel Joe Vandeleur reached the canal at Son. He rowed in a small boat across the waterway, amidst the cheering American paratroopers, to meet Brigadier General Higgins on the northern bank.

Having penetrated twenty miles into enemy territory and linked up with 101st Airborne, the Guards had every reason to believe that, with the bridge replaced overnight, the following day would see them reaching their objectives to the north. As the 101st Airborne Division were holding the next ten miles of road and, as there was no sign of counter-attack, Headquarters XXX Corps shared the Guards' optimism. However, worryingly, there was virtually no information on 1st Airborne Division's situation at Arnhem.

Wounded American paratroopers and British troops queue at a mobile NAAFI canteen that were never far behind the advancing troops.

CHAPTER FIVE

101st US AIRBORNE AT SON
The blowing of the Son Bridge and 107 Panzer Brigade's attack

Following signs to **Son en Breughel** on the **N265** leave the northern suburbs of Eindhoven. Drive the four miles to Son en Breughel and shortly after reaching the southern outskirts of the town, cross the modern replacement lift bridge over the Wilhemina Canal. Resist the temptation to park in the convenient bus stop just across the canal, as this causes offence. There is plenty of room on the parallel, local traffic, carriageway near the supermarket.

At bases in England, the 101st were briefed on their tasks. 506 PIR's initial objective, on their route south from their DZ to Eindhoven, was the Bridge at Son. Colonel Sink's Regiment was to drop on the open ground beyond the Son Forest, DZ Charlie, some three miles north-west of the Son Canal Bridge. The plan was for Major James La Padre's 1/506 to strike due south from the DZ through the Son Forest to the Wilhemina Canal and attack the Bridge from the west. This battalion was also responsible for capturing a subsidiary bridge that lay 1,400 yards to the west of the main Canal Bridge. Having assembled at their battalion RVs, 2 and 3/506 PIR were then to move down the road and cross the Canal Bridge and advance into Eindhoven. 2/506 were responsible for another subsidiary bridge 1,400 yards to the east. These objectives, up to and including Eindhoven, where 506 PIR were to have met up with the Guards, were planned to be secured before last light on 17 September.

The Drop – PM Sunday 17 September 1944
Before take-off, commanders mulled over their plans, as watched by correspondent, WB Courtney, the:
  '... *long files of the fighting skymen are waddling in their grotesque clothes, and with packs and weapons of all sizes carried on their shoulders, out to the planes. You are not prepared for their happy go lucky mood at such a moment, so*

Men of the 101st Airborne boarding a C-47 Skytrain (Dakota) for the assault on the bridges in Holland.

unlike the quiet grimness of the land infantry. They shout and wise crack and catcall. They see a handful of US nurses, trim in blue fatigue coveralls, watching them from beside the control tower, and immediately there is an outburst of whistling across the field.

C-47s carrying the 506th lifted off from Aldermaston, Captain Robert Jones commented that it,

'was a beautiful day. Amazing sight – planes could be seen forward and backward as far as I could see. The front of the air column was over Holland while the rear was over England.'

The stream of aircraft crossed the coast of liberated Belgium before turning north towards the DZ. Below the ground troops looked skywards as the throbbing of aeroengines grew into a roar as the C-47 passed overhead and the German anti-aircraft gunners ran to their positions.'

Despite the observations of WB Courtney, once in the aircraft, as the divisional historian recalls:

'The atmosphere in the C-47s was tense for there was plenty that a man could worry about. Many of the veterans, aware of what was coming, were more nervous than they had been before Normandy.'

One manifestation of nerves and, no doubt, pre-takeoff coffee, produced a tension releasing incident in one aircraft, courtesy of Staff Sergeant Charles Mitchell:

'In the plane, on the way over, we passed the bucket for that last relief. PFC Bill Barclay was last and it fell to him to throw the contents out of the door. My position was just to the rear of the open door and the prop-blast blew it back all over me. When we reached the drop zone every man went out of the ship still laughing, at my expense.'

For most, however, tension became fear, as anti-aircraft shells started bursting around the aircraft when they crossed the front-line on the Escaut Canal. In many cases, shell splinters tore through the aircraft's thin aluminium skin injuring paratroopers, who were unhooked and left in the cabin to be returned to England. In other cases, direct hits sent aircraft tumbling out of the sky with the loss of both crew and paratroopers. However, some aircraft, suffering severe damage were heroically kept on a steady course that enabled the paratroopers to jump to safety. One such example is of airforce pilot Second Lieutenant Herbert Shulman,

'He said, "Don't worry about me! I'm going to drop these

... green light go! C-47s unload their precious cargoes over Holland.

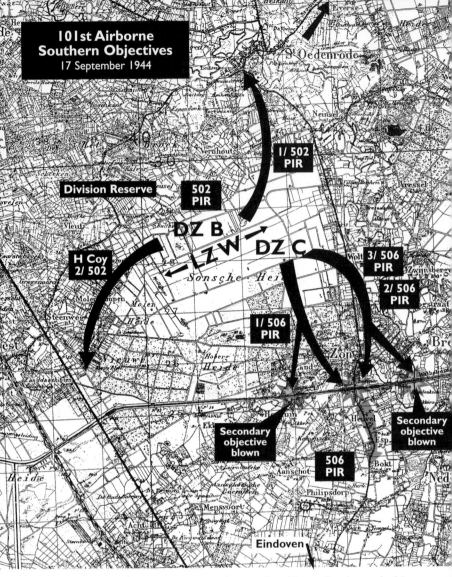

troops on the DZ." He kept his word and immediately crashed in
flames after the drop.'

There is evidence that at least four brave young pilots stayed at
the controls of their burning aircraft in order to make an
accurate drop.

The drop was recalled as 'the best ever divisional drop,
including training exercises.' Others described it as a 'Parade
ground jump', with the flat country of Holland being ' one large

The US 101st Airborne's Drop on DZ B and C at Son.

DZ'. Of the 424 C-47 aircraft used by the 101st in the first lift, sixteen were shot down (most paratroops managed to jump), 14 were badly damaged and eighty-four were damaged less severely. Including 501 PIR, who jumped on DZ Alpha to the north, 6,641 Screaming Eagles of 101st Airborne were put down in Holland in just forty minutes. This was achieved with only two percent casualties, including the inevitable landing injuries.

Son and the Bridge over the Wilhelmina Canal – Sunday 17 September 1944

The war diary of Company A, 1/506 PIR recalls:

'Thirty-five minutes after the jump, ... Capt Davis and two officers ... together with about 65 other men of the company moved from the assembly area toward the company objective. Company A had been given the principal mission of taking the main bridge across the Wilhelmina Canal, just south of Son.'

The subsidiary Bridge to the west, was to be the objective of Company C while Company B was to be battalion reserve. Still missing about forty men, who had been dropped on the other side of the DZ, Company A was soon in action. The company war diary continues:

'About 400 yards south east of the assembly point about half a squad of enemy riflemen fire on the force. However, this resistance was overcome in about five minutes and Captain Davis and his company passed on about 80 yards from the first point of contact to the south. PFC Ericson, who was scouting to the front, sighted two enemy riflemen who withdrew behind a barn when fired on. At this point, the group was about 200 yards from the bridge ... A German 88 gun opened up, firing into the trees above the heads of our troops.

ST OEDENRODE   DZ B   LANDING ZONE W   DZ C   SON   SON FOREST

The Drop Zones between St Oedenrode and the Son Forest.

> *Captain Davis urged the company forward. The enemy fire from the 88 gun increased in intensity and was joined by enemy mortars. In about fifteen minutes five men were killed and eight wounded. [The Company withdrew] 25 yards to a position in a ditch that afforded comparative cover. This was about two hours after jump time. Immediately thereafter Maj La Prade appeared and took command of the situation.'*

Men of the 101st leaving their Drop Zone areas whilst being welcomed by Dutch civilians.

Major La Prade had discovered that the subsidiary bridge, Company C's objective, had been blown several days earlier and concentrated his battalion to take his main objective.

Meanwhile, Colonel Sink and 2 and 3/506 PIR were assembling on the DZ, where apparently, groups disorientated on landing headed for battalion smoke markers on the wrong side of the DZ and found that they had joined 502 PIR. Overhead, Mustangs circled ready to fall on any identified opposition. At least two tanks that would otherwise have barred 506 PIR's route from the eastern end of the DZ were knocked out. 2nd Battalion led off, followed by Colonel Sink in his jeep, which had been in one of the first glider serials, along with the engineers. 3rd Battalion brought up the rear of the column, as it moved down the road towards Son.

Four hundred yards from the bridge, a burst of machine gun fire from a detachment of Training Regiment Herman Goering, brought the advance to a temporary halt but beyond the machine guns lay more serious opposition. Section commander of 2/506 PIR's anti-tank section, Sergeant Jack MacLean recalls that:

'A pair of 88 guns were firing directly down the street and impeding our advance and we had the first of many such commands – "Bazookas up front!"'

His section joined a Company D platoon in a right flanking move that took them within fifty metres of the enemy guns. MacLean continues:

'Pvt. Lindsey, highly skilled in his work with the weapon, moved forward into position, fired one round at the 88 nearest our group, disabling it and killing one of the Germans.'

The remainder of Company D shot up the second gun and the advance of Companys' D and E continued. The only support weapons available to cover the advance were the Regiment's medium mortars, with two rounds each having to be carried forward by an infantry soldier from the Drop Zone. At this point both 1st and 2nd Battalions were closing in on the Bridge. The divisional historian records that as:

'The 2nd Battalion moved on towards the centre bridge, its leaders wondering what had become of La Prade's battalion [who should have already taken the bridge]. ... Meanwhile, the centre was receiving rifle fire and machine gun fire from a house on the far side of the canal. The battalion began getting

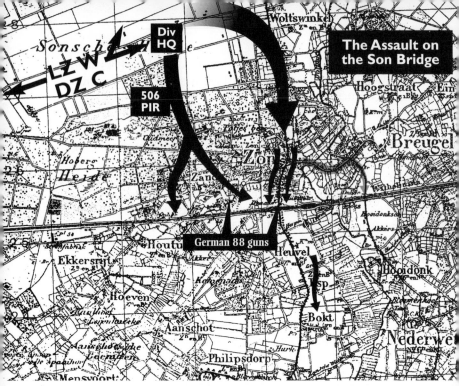

The Assault on
the Son Bridge

*casualties, about ten men being wounded at this stage. Rifle,
machine gun, bazooka and finally mortar fire was placed on the
house. It became silent. The men continued to advance. Leading
groups of all three rifle companies moved to within fifty yards of
the bank ...* [Having knocked out the 88s that had earlier
held them up] *The first men from 1st Battalion had appeared
on the right flank. Suddenly, with a roar, the bridge went up.'*

Sergeant Hugh Pritchard was one of those closest to the Bridge
when it went up.

*'We jumped back under the cover of buildings while huge
chunks of wood and other debris rained down all around us. I
had no idea I was that close to the Bridge.'*

The attempt to take the Son Bridge intact had failed. The
defenders from the Herman Goering *Kampfgruppe* had not been
panicked into blowing the bridge at the first sight of the
approaching enemy but had waited until they were sure that the
Americans would capture it. Without a *coup de main* the
attackers had lost the element of surprise and the German
defenders had ample time to prime the electronic demolition
circuits. Together, boldness and surprise combined delivers

battlefield success but, in this case, over-cautious planners who wished to avoid the Eindoven flak denied the ground troops a vital objective on the first day of the battle.

Moments after the bridge exploded, Major La Prade and members of his Tactical HQ jumped into the river and, loosing some kit in the process, swam the canal. Colonel Sink, arriving at the canal bank, was not prepared to let the lack of bridge prevent him reaching Eindhoven. He ordered 2/506 to close up to the canal and give covering fire, while 1/506 prepared to mount an immediate assault crossing across the canal. Corporal Gordon Casey spotted an old rowing boat on the opposite bank, stripped and dived into the canal and swam across to get it. His attempt to ferry part of a squad across ended in farce, as the boat foundered during the first crossing. However, on reaching the other side, Major La Prade and his swimmers, promptly attacked the house that the enemy had earlier fired from to halt 2nd Battalion's advance. With the immediate resistance disposed of, getting soldiers across the eighty foot Canal to form a bridgehead, fully occupied the 1st Battalion.

3rd Platoon, Company C, 326th Engineers, had dropped with 506 PIR in case the bridge was blown. Within three minutes of the explosion, Lieutenant Young heard the cry 'Engineers up front'. As they moved along the road into Son, they were unprepared for the enthusiastic welcome of the Dutch people, who were drawn up either side of the road waving orange flags. Apples and pears were pressed on the paratroopers but of more interest to soldiers were the cigars being handed out by the

Modern building on the canal bank at Son. On the site of this house is where the Americans were fired at from.

BRIDGE

parish priest and the glasses of beer that appeared from the rapidly opened village bars. So enthusiastic was the welcome that officers had difficulty in keeping the men moving. Once the engineers reached the canal, they found the infantry swimming across. Lieutenant Young has written,

> 'We had no engineer equipment and we had to get a footbridge across to move the entire 506th Regiment across. We had trained for many kinds of improvisation but not this. ... I sent men to find hammers, nails, boards, planks, etc. Somebody located two boats, which we placed midway from the shore to the pier. Then we made a rickety bridge that worked provided my men helped steady the infantry as they moved across. Before midnight, the entire regiment [2,000 men] had crossed. Some of my men located bigger and better planks and, in the middle of the night, replaced the rickety bridge with a fairly substantial one.'

As he was digesting the implications of the loss of the bridge, General Taylor received disturbing news from the Dutch resistance that it was possible that a significant force of Germans had occupied Eindhoven. With his infantry only slowly crossing the canal, he decided not to advance into Eindhoven and fight what could be an unequal battle. Instead, he set about forming a firm bridgehead based on Bokt, a mile and a half down the road to Eindhoven. The blowing of the Son Bridge was a cruel blow to MARKET GARDEN. Its loss caused delay in seizing Eindhoven, which took most of the following day and halted the armoured advance, while a replacement bridge was built.

Bridging the Wilhelmina Canal – Monday 18 September 1944
    The Household Cavalry Regiment, leading the Guards Armoured Division reached Son at 14.00 hours. With the help of the American Engineers and the civilian telephone network, the Royal Engineers knew the size of the problem and had bridging equipment on the way forward. By early evening, 14 Squadron RE had battled its way through traffic jams and were at work building a Bailey Bridge on abutments prepared by Company C, 326 Engineers. Lieutenant Colonel Jones, commander of the Guards Armoured Division's Royal Engineers, confidently predicted that the bridge would be complete at 06.00 hours the following morning, Tuesday 19 September 1944. Working in a fine but moonless night work progressed well and according to the HCR's historian:

A short and simple example of a Bailey Bridge. By the use of multiple sections in a wide variety of ways, these bridges were capable of taking heavy traffic and could be built very quickly.

> 'It is said that the German prisoners working for the Sappers became so infected by the urgency of their task that one inquisitive Gunner officer who came to see how things were progressing was bluntly told in English to move out of the way as he was hindering operations!'

Exactly as predicted by Lieutenant Colonel Jones, 14 Squadron and 326 Engineers completed the bridging at 06.00 hours. In less than ten hours of darkness, the Sappers had built a 100 foot class

Aerial photograph showing the destroyed bridge at Son taken at 1600 hours on 17 September.

The first tank across the newly erected Bailey Bridge at Son was a Sherman belonging to the Grenadier Guards Group.

40 Bailey Bridge over the canal. First across were the armoured cars of B Squadron 2/HCR followed by the 37 ton Shermans of the Grenadier Guards Group, who took over the lead from the Irish Guards. The route north was reported clear by the 101st Airborne Division, who had established their command post at Son and was now under command of XXX Corps. Armed with this reassuring knowledge, the Guards were able to head north towards Nijmegen at best speed. By 07.00 hours the leading tanks were passing through the small town of Veghel, having advanced ten miles in just fifty minutes, cheered as they went by the US Paratroopers who were securing the route. The breakthrough into the enemy rear seemed to have been achieved.

Attack of 107 Panzer Brigade – Dusk Tuesday 19 September 1944

Twenty-four hours after the Allied attack, German commanders were recovering from their initial confusion. Major Freiherr von Maltzahn's 107 Panzer Brigade, about to entrain, *en route* for the Eastern Front, was instead, directed towards the town of Helmond, seven miles to the east of Eindhoven. This was a freshly re-equipped and powerful armoured formation, described as 'a small but well equipped pocket Panzer division', whose principal unit was a battalion of Panther tanks. Missing from the Brigade's order of battle was the all-important Workshop Company that had gone on ahead on an earlier train. This would affect the brigade's availability of armoured vehicles over the coming days.

By late afternoon on 19 September, forty Panthers were in their concentration area in the Molenheide Woods four east of the Son Bridge. While his Brigade was preparing for their attack, von Maltzahn went forward to observe and saw a constant stream of vehicles heading north across the Son Bridge. These were the eight hundred vehicles of the Guards' unwieldy supply column, heading to Nijmegen. However, with very difficult tank country, offering only limited approaches, von Maltzahn had few options. He settled for an attack by a small body of tanks and infantry, supported by the bulk of his armour firing high explosive to make up for the lack of artillery. Their mission was to block the route and destroy the vital bridge across the canal in a surprise attack. This would isolate the airborne divisions and the bulk of Guards Armoured Division from the mass of XXX Corps who were still waiting for space on the road north.

At 101st's Divisional Command Post, which had been established in school buildings between the village of Son and the bridge, reports of enemy tanks started to arrive from Dutch

107 Panzer Brigade move speedily but cautiously south towards its objective.

sources. At the same time came situation reports from XXX Corps that the flanking corps' advance was progressing well. Consequently, the 101st were unsure who the tanks belonged to until, as Corporal Shoemaker described:

'*about 17.00 hours I remember distinctly two Dutchmen riding up hell-bent-for-leather on their bicycles from down the canal bank to the east. They hopped off and started talking excitedly in broken English. The news they had was that there were five or six German tanks coming up along the canal bank and they were very close in.... We were pretty well spread out on that side of the road. All we could do was sit there and wait for them.*'

The defences to the east of Son were indeed thin, as a battle at Best, to the west of the Son Forest, had sucked in the Division's reserves. In close proximity to the Bailey Bridge was a platoon of infantry and some engineers; while further out on the north-eastern side were the glider pilots. The Son Bridge was highly vulnerable but, with twenty miles of road for the 101st to guard, this was inevitable.

107 Panzer Brigade were not the only troops manoeuvring to the east of Eindhoven. Having secured the city during the previous evening, the American 506 Parachute Infantry pushed their defensive out into the surrounding country. Company E 2nd Battalion, accompanied by Cromwells of 15/19 Hussars established themselves in Nuenen, about four miles north-east of the city. In the late afternoon, patrols were tasked to check out the woods beyond the village. Suddenly, Private Jack Matthews, riding on the turret of a Cromwell yelled above the noise of tracks and engine: '*Kraut tanks! Kraut tanks!*' In the close Molenheide country, a patrol had bumped into 107 Panzer Brigade's flank protection screen at a range of four hundred metres. The German armoured patrols were covering the move forward by the Brigade's main-body in the attack on the Son Bridge.

In a moment, the paratroopers had leapt off the tanks while the tank commanders and gunners sought targets amongst the trees and bushes. Nothing happened. One of the other Cromwells moved up to help. Sergeant Martin climbed up onto the tank to point out a target that was hidden little more than a hundred metres away. The tank edged forward, so the American paratrooper cautioned the British commander who laconically

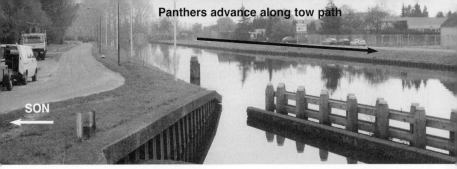

Panthers advance along tow path

SON

The section of canal today where 107 Panzer Brigade attacked the Son Bailey Bridge Bridge on the evening of 19 September 1944.

replied, 'I caunt see him old boy and if I caunt see him, I caunt very well shoot him'. Sargent Martin jumped off the tank with the words 'You'll see him damm soon'. Almost immediately, he was off the tank, it was hit by an armour-piercing round from a Panther and the Cromwell burst into flames. The crew bailed out including the gunner who had lost both his legs. With the gears still engaged, the burning vehicle rolled onwards but it failed to distract the gunner manning the 75mm mounted in the Panther's turret and a second Cromwell was left burning. The paratroopers and remaining tanks withdrew to Nuenen pursued by the Panzers. After a sharp fight at dusk, the Allied patrols broke clear and withdrew to the suburbs of Eindhoven under cover of darkness.

Meanwhile, the main effort of 107 Panzer Brigade was approaching the Son Bridge. Sharing the same problems as the Allies of finding routes across country for the forty-four ton Panthers, progress had been slow. The German tanks were preceded by dismounted infantry from 1034 Grenadier

A 107 Panzer Brigade Panther knocked out on the approach to the Son Bridge.

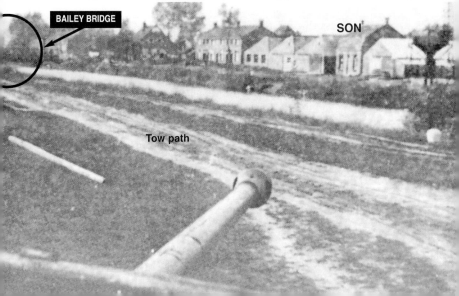

BAILEY BRIDGE

SON

Tow path

Regiment moving stealthily towards Son from the south-east. Their immediate objective was the subsidiary bridge half a mile to the east of the main crossing. It was a rude shock to find that it had been blown by their own forces several days before. Consequently, as von Maltzahn could not deploy to the south of the canal and because the Dommel lay across his path, he was forced to strike east, along the canal towpath. This gave him no room for manoeuvre. Also, thwarted was the German intention to co-ordinate von Maltzahn's attack, with a similar assault from the west by 59th Division, as this division was still arriving and was not ready to take part. Even without support, 107 Panzer Brigade's attack nearly succeeded.

In response to the threat of German armour, several patrols, led by divisional staff officers, were sent out to locate the enemy. Lieutenant Colonel Ned Moore, divisional G1 (the staff officer responsible for personnel and discipline) led one of the patrols. He took with him members of divisional HQ and attached a bazooka team from the infantry platoon guarding the bridge. The divisional historian records how:

'The group had proceeded along the canal for about two hundred yards when they saw movement in the trees along the canal three hundred yards to the front. A well-camouflaged tank burst from the trees and headed along the canal bank. It opened fire on the bridge soon setting a truck on fire on the bridge.'

This was an ammunition vehicle from Q Battery 21st Anti-Tank Regiment Royal Artillery. It proceeded to burn furiously, with exploding ammunition illuminating the scene and blocking XXX Corps' route north. Von Maltzahn had achieved his first aim, through surprise but in the gathering dusk and close country his tanks were now at a disadvantage.

News of the attack reached divisional HQ about the same time as arrival of enemy shells in the HQ buildings, which made the enemy's presence all too obvious to General Taylor's staff. German tanks giving fire support and advancing on Son from the east had crossed north of the canal on one of several bridges north of Molenheide. Meanwhile, back on the towpath, Pte McCarthy engaged the tank with his bazooka, missing with the first two rounds and the third hit but failed to stop it, having probably hit the tank's thick frontal armour. Cpl Shoemaker described the enemy tank's approach

'...he looked about the size of a house! That is the one that

Paratroopers of 101st Airborne examine a Panther tank, knocked out by a 57mm anti-tank gun during 107 Panzer Brigade's attack on the Son Bridge.

mauled a truck on the bridge. It got kind of confusing. We didn't know if it was a big force coming our way. ... We couldn't do a helluva lot about it. Jim Hoenscheidt was in a very precarious position ... he threw a partly eaten apple towards the German infantry. They thought it was a grenade and ducked. This gave him an opportunity to get out of his predicament.'

A nearby haystack was set on fire, which illuminated the scene. The leading Panther continued to advance on the bridge, followed by five others, scattering the American defenders, who lacking anti-tank weapons were defenceless. The tanks were however separated from their accompanying infantry by small arms fire. The rifle and machine gun fire was heaviest from the cover of the school walls, where the divisional HQ personnel were firing for all they were worth. The Panthers' turrets traversed inexorably right and the 75mm guns sent five HE rounds crashing into the school building. Seemingly impervious in their tanks, yet with limited visibility, the Germans were unable to deal with the paratroopers, without infantry support.

The stalemate was broken by the arrival of a 57mm anti-tank gun rushed forward by Battery B, 81st Anti-Tank Battalion, who had arrived by glider only hours before. Captain Alphons Gueymard wrote:

'Upon reaching the bridge we observed a large tank on the

*south side of the canal, due east of the bridge. We were able to get
an anti-tank gun beside a house and fired at the tank which was
moving along the levee. Our first round* [in the side of the
tank] *disabled the tank and the crew jumped out and
disappeared. Several other rounds were fired for good measure.'*

The destruction of a second tank by a bazooka prompted the
remaining German tanks to follow the panzer grenadiers and
withdraw to the east. The crisis had passed but chaos rained on
the road, which was already earning its reputation as *'Hell's
Highway'*, rather than the official British nickname for XXX
Corps' main supply route – *'Club Route'*. As the fighting died
down, further reinforcements arrived, this time from 1/327
Glider Infantry Regiment, who took up defensive positions
around the bridge.

The 101st Airborne were surprised that the enemy had not
pressed home his advantage. However, from a German point of
view, the attack was over very poor ground for tanks, in
darkness without coordinated infantry support, against an
enemy who did not run but stood and fought, despite the fact
he only had small-arms. That night von Maltzahn and the rest
of 107 Panzer Brigade was to get precious little rest as the
infantry and armour had, in the darkness, withdrawn in
opposite directions and regrouping was a protracted affair.
Although the attack by 107 Panzer Brigade may not have
physically blocked the road for long, the impact on XXX Corps'
movement north was felt well into the night. The HCR who
were picketing the route report a typical incident.

'... a D.R. [dispatch rider] *appeared, covered in mud.
Slowing down and only pausing long enough to shout "There's
a pocket Panzer division on the road moving south towards you
and orders are that you have got to turn around", he was off
again in a flash.*

*Before he could be grabbed by authority he had dashed down
a large part of the column, spreading his alarming message.
There was no wireless with the lorries, and unfortunately a batch
of R.A.S.C. vehicles took him at his word and, without more ado,
turned about and made off at speed back the way they had come.
... Eventually the lorries were collected together in a field near
Aalst and they rejoined the convoy.'*

Commentators dismissing enemy action as a reason for the slow
advance of XXX Corps have consistently failed to appreciate the

A Guards Armoured Division truck destroyed during the bombing of Eindoven.

true extent of the disruption caused by enemy action on the flanks of Hell's Highway. Many of the troops on the Corridor were from supporting arms and services who would not normally expect to find themselves in the front line. Though 'disappointing', the truck drivers' reaction to the enemy's presence is understandable.

The Eindhoven Air-Raid

Compounding XXX Corps' problem and adding further chaos to Club Route, the enemy launched a raid by seventy aircraft on Eindhoven, shortly after dark. The Germans had been quick to exploit the Allies' loss of air supremacy over the

Dutch rescue workers in Eindhoven after the German bombing of the city. Note the wooden clogs.

battle area, caused by a combination of the distance from the UK and Normandy, poor air space co-ordination and the deteriorating weather. The air raids opened with flares that enabled pilots to identify their targets. It has been suggested that the accuracy of the raid was due to the *Luftwaffe's* use of pilots who were familiar with Eindhoven; having only recently abandon the City's airfield. In ten minutes, a part of the Philips factory was on fire and six ammunition trucks had received direct hits and were blazing. As the shells in the trucks exploded, the inferno spread to other vehicles carrying fuel and small arms ammunition. The ensuing blockage caused considerable delay to the forward movement of the Guard's vital combat supplies. Private Siddney Brown of the Royal Army Service Corps recalls how:

'We'd been stopped in the streets since before dark. Most of us were in the houses for an eat and a drink with the Dutch families, when the Hun bombers came over. We went down with them [the Dutch] to the cellars, where we stayed until the heavy crumps of the bombs had stopped. When we came up buildings and trucks were burning. There was nothing we could do until the worst of the fire had burnt the trucks out. Then we pushed the wrecks to one side. My truck miraculously survived and now with a co-driver, I was on the road before dawn. It was a long night and I was tireder than I had ever been before or since.'

Son Bridge, Dawn Wednesday 20 September 1944

Early on 20 September, XXX Corps traffic was again moving north in a frustratingly slow and seemingly endless column. Vehicles were stopping and starting, as numerous large and heavily laden vehicles queued to negotiate choke points and partial blockages caused by broken down or knocked out vehicles.

The flow of vehicles northwards was not to continue uninterrupted for long. Major von Maltzahn's attack the previous evening had nearly succeeded and without another approach having been identified, he decided to use the same route. Again, 107 Panzer Brigade's move to their attack positions was covered by the noise of XXX Corps traffic on Club Route and early autumnal mist. However, in 1/327 PIR's outpost line Private George Mullins recalls,

'During the night you could hear tanks moving some hundred yards away to the east. "No sweat, it must be our own tanks – the Germans couldn't be that close".'

Confirmation of the enemy's presence came at dawn, when, south-east of the bridge, an Anglo American Jeep patrol found themselves surrounded by marching troops. A British colonel turned hopefully to his American companion, 'These are some of your chaps aren't they?' The paratrooper replied 'No, they are Germans. We'd better try and get out of here in a hurry!' which they did, engines screaming in reverse, under enemy fire.

Forewarned of the attack from the south-east, Company C 1/327 GIR were stood-to and other troops in the area rushed to the bridge. 'The need for troops became extreme, thirty company clerks and other headquarters men ... were rushed into the fight.'

Even so, the Americans' outposts were overwhelmed by German infantry from 1034 Grenadier Regiment, who were leading, with the tanks supporting. The Panzers were again suffering limitations on manoeuvre imposed by the ground. In addition, as the divisional historian put it, 'The 81st's anti-tank guns kept the enemy tanks at a respectful distance.'

The Germans had managed to assemble a greater number of troops but the attack fared less well against the now properly defended bridge. The arrival of the ten Cromwells from 15/19 Hussars and battery of British self-propelled 25-pounder artillery, both attached to the 101st, swung the balance in favour of the Allies. Unfortunately for the Allies, as the British armour manoeuvred to bring fire down on the Germans, the leading tank hit a row of mines that had been hastily laid by the Americans during the night. However, the volume of small arms and anti-tank fire being put down by the Americans and the lack of German artillery support meant that the enemy were unable to press home their attack. 107 Panzer Brigade withdrew, leaving four Panthers burning and the ground littered with German bodies. The two attacks had cost von Maltzahn six tanks or ten percent of his valuable panzers.

A part of a temporary US cemetery at Wolfswinkel near Son testifies to the intensity of the fighting in the area.

CHAPTER SIX

BEST – THE UNPLANNED BATTLE
An unequal battle on the flanks

In common with Eindhoven and Son, the urban area around Best is far more extensive than it was in 1944 and a major highway bisects the countryside. However the topography of the woods, canals and minor roads have changed little. The area is definitely worth a visit. Leave the Son Bridge heading towards Nijmegen. **Turn left at the traffic lights** in the centre of Son onto the **N620** towards **Best**. To reach the Son memorial turn right on Europalaan. Return to the **N620**, follow the road through the houses into the wood and cross under the new motorway. Take the first left after the motorway onto **Hoberglaan**. Follow this road down to the canal, along the canal bank and turn right just before the Motorway Bridge. Park near the Joe Man Memorial.

The Son Liberation Memorial located on Europalaan.

The battle around the small town of Best was the result of Major General Taylor's wish that a significant bridge, three miles to the west of the main axis, should be secured, as insurance against the loss of the Son Bridge. However, Best was destined to become a magnet for the opposing forces and the scale of the fighting escalated over several days.

The parachute drop of 502 PIR went remarkably well but even so, 1/502 PIR was dropped by error amongst 506 PIR on DZ B. Assembling after the drop inevitably takes time, as a member of 101st Airborne described a typical landing:

'When you hit the ground and stop, all you feel is gratitude for still being alive. You have trouble getting out of your harness. If you hear firing, you hop into the nearest ditch. You are suddenly aware of five hundred other parachutists dropping through the sky right at you and you start dodging. By this time, you have lost all sense of direction. So, even if you remember that the assembly point is in the south-east corner of the field, it does no good. You get out a compass. You study landmarks and try to remember your briefing sessions.

A smoke signal has gone off somewhere. Everyone seems to be moving in one direction. You join a group. When you get there,

you find out that it is the right battalion but the wrong company.
Someone says you are supposed to be four hundred yards south,
across a brook. On the way there you see a buddy with a bad
ankle and stop to help him. Finally arriving you find your
platoon leader. What a relief to be back with your own crowd.'

Having assembled, General Taylor was to retain most of 502 PIR
in the area of the DZs in order to secure the area for subsequent
lifts. 1/502 PIR was, however, to occupy St Oedenrode, a small
town on the northern edge of the DZ B, leaving the majority of
the Regiment to be, in effect, a divisional reserve. The bridges at
Best had been of no interest to General Sir Miles Dempsey
(Commander Second British Army), who when briefed, wished
to focus only on the narrow corridor north. General Taylor,
however, felt that he could safely afford to detach a single company of 3/502 PIR to secure these alternative bridges.

Captain Robert Jones's Company H, reinforced by 3rd
Platoon, Company C, 326 Engineers and a section of machine
guns from Battalion Headquarters, was tasked to take and hold
Best's road and rail bridges across the Wilhelmina Canal.
Leaving the DZ was a slow business, with the paratroopers
carefully climbing or crawling under barbed wire fences that
divided the DZ into paddocks. Captain Jones recording that on
countless exercises in England, the message 'do not destroy
civilian property' was drummed into them said that:

'This went on until Lt Colonel Robert Cole, the battalion
commander, in a very forceful and clear rhetoric told them to
"Cut the God-dammed wire and quit wasting time!" This was
done quickly and the battalion moved out more rapidly'

Captain Jones had pointed out the steeple of Best's church as a
reference point on Company H's right flank. However, in the
belts of trees and small woods, the leading soldiers became disorientated and veered to the right towards their reference point
in Best rather than away from it, towards the bridges. As many
soldiers will testify, reference points in difficult country tend to
have a strangely magnetic effect! Emerging on open ground, little more than four hundred metres from Best, Company H came
under fire. Pressing forward, they were about to overcome the
small groups of German defenders. However, a convoy of
twelve trucks, halted in its journey south to the front line, dis-
gorged three hundred infantrymen from another *kampfgruppe* of
General Chill's 59th Division. The balance of force had swung

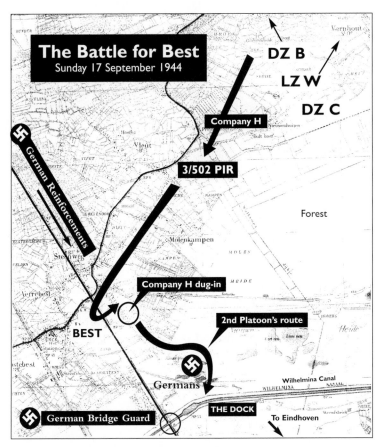

The Battle for Best
Sunday 17 September 1944

DZ B

LZ W

DZ C

Company H

3/502 PIR

German Reinforcements

Forest

Company H dug-in

2nd Platoon's route

BEST

Germans

Wilhelmina Canal

German Bridge Guard

THE DOCK

To Eindhoven

decisively in favour of the Germans. At this point, Lieutenant Colonel Cole, who had been monitoring progress reports on his Battalion radio net, ordered Captain Jones to send 2nd Platoon, his engineers and machine guns to take the bridge. He did not want Company H to be deflected from its mission by becoming sucked into a battle at Best. Denuded of men Captain Jones withdrew his remaining two platoons several hundred metres to the wood lines between Best and the DZ. Here they dug foxholes and fought for the night with mounting casualties against probing German attacks.

2nd Platoon, led by Lieutenant Edward

Best church. It's steeple was used as reference point for the right flank of Company H.

107

The modern bridge across the Wilhemina Canal at Best today.

Wierzbowski, started a cautious advance through the western edge of the Son Forest, which was made up of plantations of young pine trees (fifty-five years later, now mature and ready for felling). The Germans had positioned machine guns to fire along the firebreaks. According to the 101st's historian:

> *'Wishing to preserve every man he had, Wierzbowski insisted that each lane be checked, and those under fire be taken in individual rushes. As an added precaution, he had the entire column swing seventy-five yards to the left away from the machine guns. His men chafed at these delays, for they were eager to get to the bridges. ... Darkness fell while they were picking their way through the woods, and with the coming of darkness, it began to rain.'*

Lieutenant Charles More, commander of the engineer platoon, accompanied Lieutenant Wierzbowski and recalls:

> *'Moving through the dense pine trees in single file in the dark started the problem. The German machine guns continually cut the line of march. I learned later that many of the men drifted back to battalion headquarters.'*

Eventually, the much-reduced group of paratroopers emerged onto the canal bank some 1,000 yards east of the bridge. They made their way towards the Road Bridge until a fenced dock blocked their way. In the words of the divisional historian:

> *'Willing to gamble, he* [Lieutenant Wierzbowski] *led the group along a wet and slippery catwalk suspended around the derricks out over the canal. No flares went off while they were*

thus exposed. Regaining the bank, they continued west, feeling their way in the darkness.'

Closing in on the bridge, Lieutenant Wierzbowski's patrol penetrated the German defences. This, however, only became apparent when a sentry returning to his post walked past the prone Americans. The paratroopers remained where they were until an exchange of fire and grenades started between the Germans across the canal and 2nd Platoon's main body to their rear. Under cover of the commotion, Lieutenant Wierzbowski withdrew and took the remaining members of his command back to the edge of the wood.

The following morning, 2nd Platoon shot up groups of Germans attempting to withdraw through their part of the wood and witnessed the Germans blowing the bridge at 11.00 hours. Shortly afterwards, an armoured car from 2/HCR, along with a scout car, appeared on the opposite canal bank from the direction of Son and bumped the German position. They withdrew to a safe distance, from where they machine-gunned the Germans, who promptly withdrew. Persuaded by the British to stay where he was while they attempted to get in contact with the 101st, Lieutenant Wierzbowski's problems were far from over, as 'the Son Forest was still alive with groups of aggressive Germans'.

Meanwhile, the previous evening, Colonel Michaelis had also been monitoring Company H's progress and the arrival of Germans in the area of Best. It was clear to him that there was a threat developing on what was an important enemy reinforcement route and that he needed to reinforce Captain Jones. Just before dark the remaining two companies of 3/502 PIR were tasked to join the battle. They approached to within a mile of Best but they came under heavy artillery and mortar fire. Unable to move forward without unacceptable casualties, the two companies and Battalion Headquarter dug in. In front of them was Sergeant Joe Ludwig, with Company H: 'during the night, we were getting the hell shot out of us' and 2nd Platoon was given up as lost.

During the night, Major Klauck's 'battalion' numbering one hundred and fifty *Wehrmacht* infantry from 347th Division, was just one of four units directed to the battle. In his case, his convoy had been taken off the road at Boxtel and directed to Best. He recalled during questioning after the battle that:

'I was assured that these were the personal orders of General der Fallschirmtrupen Student and I had to obey. In the dark, we took up positions outside of Best with difficulty. The night was not quiet. There was quite a bit of shooting, as artillery arrived and registered on the enemy.'

Monday 18 September 1944 – The Battle Grows

During the night, 2/502 PIR was the Division's reserve and spent the night preparing to support 506 PIR in Eindhoven. Therefore, it came as a surprise when, in the early hours, orders came to move to the relief of Lieutenant Colonel Cole's hard-pressed 3rd Battalion at Best. Lieutenant Colonel Chappuis, commanding 2nd Battalion, was given instructions to attack on 3/503 PIR's northern or right flank and then to swing south along the axis of the road towards the bridge. Colonel Cole would give fire support from machine guns and medium mortars, with ammunition being transported forward by Dutch farm carts. In reply the Germans had 88mm guns, 105mm artillery and numerous Spandaus.

As 2/502 PIR were moving back across the DZ towards Best, 3/505 PIR's battle intensified as the dawn rose. The regimental MARKET GARDEN Report recorded the deteriorating situation:

'Action began at about 0520, on 18th September, when the enemy opened fire with automatic weapons on the battalions' positions on the front and left flank. It became heavier throughout the day, with artillery and mortar fire supporting and augmenting the fire of small arms and 20mm AA gunfire. ... In the morning, the enemy made two determined attacks supported by heavy artillery and mortar concentrations. These were repulsed with heavy losses to the enemy. However, during the morning, many casualties were caused by infiltrating enemy and heavy concentrations of fire poured into the pine growths in which the battalion had taken up positions.'

Attempts by 3/502 PIR to establish roadblocks on the main road were short lived and 'they were overrun by numerically superior enemy, causing them to withdraw south east'. Pressure was relieved at about 10.00 hours when 2/502 PIR arrived on the right flank, advancing with its three companies deployed in line.

In 1944 the ground that 2/502 PIR had to cross was not only

A crashed Waco CG-4A (Hadrian) glider is being cleared of injured soldiers and equipment after a heavy landing.

completely flat but open as well, with but few farm buildings and clumps of trees to give cover from either view or fire. However, in a remarkable example of infantry fire and manoeuvre, the battalion moved onto the open ground at the outskirts of Best under heavy enemy fire. The divisional history describes the advance:

'The Dutch had been haying and the fields ahead were full of piles of uncollected hay. That was the only concealment. From left to right the line rippled forward in perfect order and with perfect discipline, each group of men dashing to the next pile as their turn came. It was as if the piles were concrete. But machine gun fire cut into them, sometimes setting the hay afire, sometimes wounding or killing the men behind them. That did not stop anyone except the dead and wounded.' See map page 113

However, the battalion was taking such heavy casualties that Lieutenant Colonel Chappuis halted the advance and pulled his battalion back, taking such wounded as they could manage with them. Coming into line with 3/502 PIR they reorganized.

Major Klauck records the American advance as a counter-attack:

'The enemy advanced across the fields towards the road and we fired at them rapidly. They came close and I had to send out Feldwebel Dorn to keep our [men in] position. The Americans stopped and withdrew. As we were still close, we could do little for the enemy wounded in front of us.'

At this point, much needed air support arrived in the form of Thunderbolts P-47s, whose airfields to the west had now cleared of mist. However, their first strafing attacks caught 3/502 in its position on the edge of the wood. Out came the orange air identification panels and smoke grenades. The aircraft broke off the attack but Lieutenant Colonel Cole stood up to get a better view of the situation and was hit in the head by an enemy shot from a nearby house, killing him instantly. Cole was a highly regarded CO and his death shook his men. However, shortly afterwards one of the battalion's machine guns killed a German running from the house. The Screaming Eagles like to think they had their revenge on the man who shot Cole. To return to the air strike, the regimental report records the:

> '... aircraft strafed and bombed the enemy at very close quarters as the enemy had advanced to within one hundred yards of our battalion lines. This support, which was the first that the battalion had received, resulted in the enemy attack being repulsed with heavy losses in troops and equipment.'

While the fighting was going on Corporal Pete Santini, back at 2/502's command post, described the arrival of the Division's sorely needed support elements:

> 'About 1450 hours, gliders began to come in. We were right smack in the field where they were going to land. Wave after wave, they came in and landed. It was an awe-inspiring sight. The men in the front lines were unable to enjoy this beautiful show of air supremacy [to their rear] but I'm sure the enemy must have felt some fear'

He was not wrong. Major Klauck is recorded to have said in his interrogation that,

> 'the arrival of the enemy gliders was a blow to the mind. It hit all of us. From knowing that we were to win this battle, in a moment we were destined to be the losers.'

The Germans made no more attacks that day, although in the woods, the two sides remained at close quarters and patrols fought sharp low level encounter actions.

Sensing a change in the situation, at 17.00 hours Colonel Michaelis ordered 2/502 to renew the attack on the bridge, which he thought to be still standing. Lieutenant Colonel Chappuis led his battalion's advance about 1,000 yards towards the bridge, clearing the enemy who had been harassing 3/502

PIR for most of the day in the process. However, they were halted short of their objective by fire from 88mm guns on the opposite bank of the canal. 2/502 PIR were now positioned on the edge of the wood between 3rd Battalions positions and the bridge. However, by this stage, both sides had fought themselves to a standstill and they halted to lick their wounds and prepare to renew the battle in the morning.

Tuesday 19 September 1944 – Victory and Defeat

By last light on 18 September, the Guards Armoured Division's main body had closed up to the Wilhelmina Canal and other 101st objectives were secure. This released tanks and additional paratroopers, with which, General Taylor reinforced 502 PIR in its unequal battle at Best. The bloody fighting of the previous days had not, however, been in vain as the fighting sucked in 'enemy reinforcements to Best from all over the Divisional area'. In doing so, though 'that was scarcely apparent

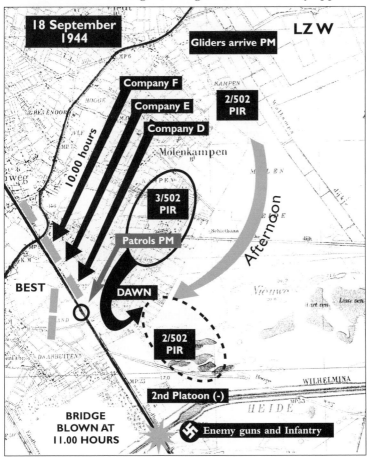

to the 502nd at the time' they had made a significant contribution to the link up between the British and Americans. By closing the Boxtel – Eindhoven road and forcing the enemy to blow the Best Canal bridge, they had prevented a German reinforcement of Eindhoven. If fresh troops had reached Eindhoven in any strength, it would have been very difficult to overcome them and, as the Guards found, routes around the city could not sustain armoured traffic.

As the battle continued to escalate on Tuesday 19 September, with General Taylor's reinforcements came the assistant divisional commander, Brigadier General Higgins, who took over coordination of the battle. His task force was to 'clear up once and for all the Best situation'. The first reinforcements to arrive were 2 and 3/327 GIR. British tanks from B and C Squadrons 15/19 Hussars and a battery of self-propelled artillery from 86 (Hertfordshire Yeomanry) Field Regiment RA followed them. On crossing the Son Bridge, the British had come under General Taylor's command at 11.00 hours. Meanwhile, 502 PIR's battle had resumed at first light, with 2nd Battalion resuming its attack on the bridge. Private First Class Parmley of Company F, 2/502 PIR, was in position:

See map
page 117
'about 150 yards east and parallel to the highway running north from the canal to Best ... The Germans were dug in on the east side of the highway. It was still dark and we were waiting for daylight to begin our attack... I recall waiting in the dark for the order to attack ... At the same time I saw Germans coming out of the buildings along the highway on the west side. The machine gunner next to me opened up. We all opened fire about the same time up and down the line. ... I had fired about three of four clips when I heard the order to attack.'

The attackers came under heavy fire from the area of the bridge and from the southern side of the canal. Private Parmley was looking for cover and 'I saw a little indentation about two inches deep where a mortar round had probably hit. It looked like the Grand Canyon to me so I dived in'. Taking cover the paratroopers saw that their objective had already been blown. In the pause that followed, while receiving orders to pull back to their original positions, a German, company strength, counter-attack came through the area 2/502 PIR had vacated and caught Company G, 3/502nd in the flank. In close-quarter fighting, the

**Lt. Col, A.D. Taylor,
Commanding Officer
15/19 Hussars**

**General Higgins, Assistant
Commander 101st
Airborne**

paratroopers of Company G held their own until 2nd Battalion returned and drove the enemy off. Reoccupying their previous position, 2/502 PIR was attacked twice more but both times the enemy were beaten off.

American historians have likened the battle that the 101st fought in Holland to the Indian Wars. With few troops and a large area to cover there were no coherent front lines and consequently plenty of gaps and open flanks. The battle was inevitably a matter of speed of thought and action. An incident on the morning of the 19th exemplifies this.

'Lt Col Ray Allen moved the 3rd [327 GIR] out as soon as he learned of the assignment, then he turned it over to his executive officer and hurried ahead to the 502nd's CP. Looking for it he stumbled on a group of two hundred Germans marching south to reinforce those in the Best area. They opened fire on him. Escaping with nothing worse than a hit on a K-ration box in his

pocket, he hastened back to his battalion column to deploy it quickly enough to destroy his enemy group. But the Germans sensed danger and gave up their formation to hurry on as fast as they could. Three times the 3rd Battalion hit them and each time they were a little late. Seventy-five of the rear stragglers were captured and some were killed.'

Brigadier General Higgins's force was eventually assembled, having given out the following plan. 2/327 GIR was to clear the forest of the many groups of Germans known to be in the area, from the Oud Meer in the centre of the forest westward towards 502 PIR's positions. Caught between the two forces the Germans would be killed or captured. In the centre, 502 PIR was to renew the attack towards the bridge site, with the support of the Cromwell tanks of B Squadron 15/19 Hussars. On the northern flank, 3/327 GIR's task was to project the western end of LZ W which was to be used by gliders at 15.00 hours and to prevent the Germans in Best attacking 502 PIR in the rear. C Squadron 15/19 Hussars was to accompany 3/327 GIR. As the Hussar's regimental historian recorded:

'Co-operation with the Americans was not easy; there had been little time to get together beforehand and naturally each of us found the methods of the other not easily intelligible. But this strangeness wore off during the next two days.'

PFC Richard Ladd, with HQ 502 PIR was amongst the first members of his regiment to encounter the British.

'Around noon we became conscious of a sound of armour approaching from the DZ. Enemy fire abruptly slackened. A lone British major [OC B Squadron] with a scarlet cloth cap on his head and a white lanyard running to his sidearm, strode into the woods and enquired loudly as to the location of the regimental CO. Someone responded quickly, "He's over there in that hole." The strange officer appeared to be seven feet tall from my humble vantage point. A brief conference with Colonel John Michaelis was followed by a throaty roar as six Cromwells and one Challenger tank [a Cromwell mounting a larger turret with a 17-pounder gun] advanced along the road parallel to the wood line.'

To the south of Best, Major Klauck had also heard the sound of the tanks:

'Officers had been sent forward to repair morale and to lead attacks on the Americans. ... The sound of panzers coming from

116

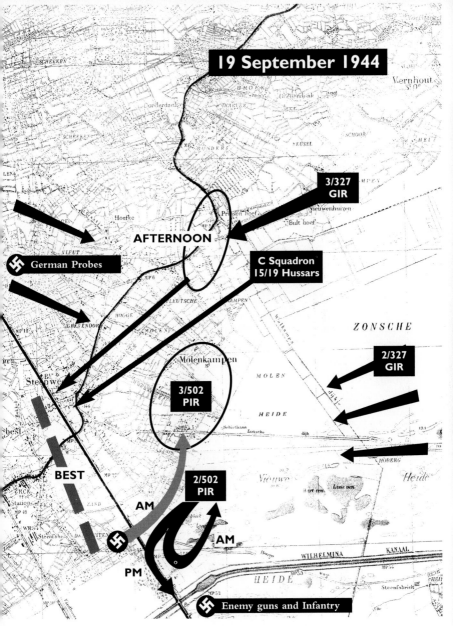

19 September 1944

3/327 GIR

AFTERNOON

C Squadron 15/19 Hussars

German Probes

ZONSCHE

2/327 GIR

3/502 PIR

BEST

2/502 PIR

AM

AM

PM

Enemy guns and Infantry

the east was a blow that we could not recover from, as we all knew that they must be yours and that it was all over for us. Soldiers were looking to their rear and we had radio reports from forward elements, telling us that the front was breaking and soldiers were surrendering.'

117

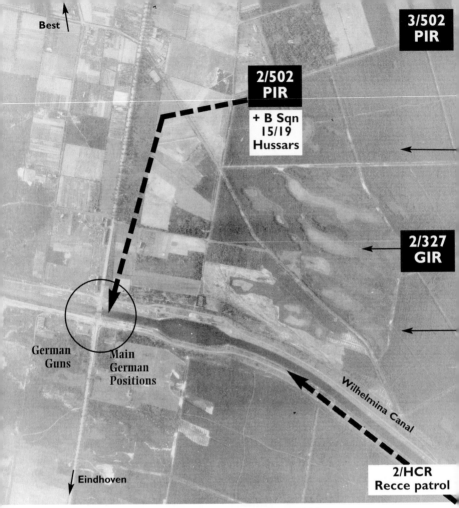

The final attack on the site of the blown bridge at Best.

As B Squadron's leading troops deployed between the forest edge and the road, the American paratroopers began to move forward. Private First Class Parmley, still in the front-line with 2/502 PIR recalled:

'When the English Cromwells reached our lines, it seemed everyone leaped out of their holes as if ejected by some force at the same time. We were all yelling and were going to charge but the tank commander was a very calm person and said, "Let's not be hasty lads, perhaps we can give Jerry something to think about." He fired the big gun. It looked like an air burst just in front of the building on the highway. There were a few white flags but

*not many. He fired again. This brought results. The Germans on
the left started surrendering as the tank moved across our front
to the right of the trees that ran down to the highway and fired
again... They started surrendering all up and down the line...'*

The Company F log records that,

*'14.30... Enemy starts surrendering in bunches, running
across open fields to our position. Some were machine-gunned by
their own troops'.*

Major Klauck was there on the opposite side:

*'I left my command post to go forward and hold the men.
Across the road, tanks were moving [south] towards the Canal.
Then more tanks appeared at the corner of the wood and opened
fire on my positions. We replied with machine-guns but platoons
to the left and right started to run or surrender as your tanks and
infantry came close. I ran to stop them surrendering but it was
too late and I was taken prisoner.'*

Major Klauck was just one of many prisoners. Private Santini
described how,

*'We held our fire and allowed as many to surrender as
wanted. These were lined up and thoroughly searched for
concealed weapons. I estimate there were between 500 and 600 of
them. About twice as many of them as there were of us, but they
still surrendered'.*

All, however, did not go the way of the Allies. 502 PIR's after-
action report details how:

*'During the height of the battle, a group of about fifty enemy
penetrated the right flank and were advancing from the rear
towards the regimental command post before they were
discovered. They were engaged by the command post personnel
and routed with considerable loss. By 17.30 hours, all enemy
resistance had ceased and the bridge area was under firm control.
The regiment immediately established a defensive position to
protect it.'*

B Squadron had a little more work to do and cleared, with fire,
a variety of enemy guns, including a German artillery battery on
the other side of the Canal.

2/327 GIR's advance progressed well but clearing woods
and forests is always slow and costly, with short-range
encounters resulting in numerous casualties. However, by late
afternoon the Son Forest was finally cleared of Germans. To the
north, 3/327 GIR's attack was spearheaded by Company G,

A Cromwell tank on Hell's Highway.

supported by tanks of C Squadron positioned themselves astride the road. Enemy mortar fire was a particular nuisance to the parachute infantry and it was strongly suspected that the Germans had an OP in Best's church steeple, so accurate was the fire. 3/327 GIR were soon in position astride the road taking up all round defence but no attempt was made to enter Best, which 'was ominously quiet'. However, soon snipers joined the enemy mortars in making life unpleasant for the American glidertroops.

502 PIR's after-action report revealed that:

'...the area covered by the regiment on the 17th, 18th and 19th September, had contained 2,500 enemy troops. Of these, 1042 were captured, and an estimated 800 were killed. This figure was reported by a British unit, which later occupied the area and buried the dead. Reinforcing his normal complement of machine

guns and mortars, the enemy had eight 88mm guns, two 75mm anti-tank guns and five 20mm anti-aircraft guns.

Casualties in the regiment were particularly heavy ... 29 officers and 420 enlisted men'.

Best was still strongly held and 51st (Highland) Division finally took it a month later, after considerable difficulties. In the meantime, 327 GIR were to take over defence of the Best sector from 502 PIR. However, the paratroopers could not be extracted until 377 Artillery Battalion concentrated its fire against German batteries and silenced them long enough for the battalions to carry out a relief in place. 502 PIR were taken into reserve after three days in action. They were positioned in the St Oedenrode area where there were ominous indications of increasing enemy strength.

Retrace your steps to **Sonseweg**, heading towards **Son**. To the right is the memorial to Joe Mann, who earned the Congressional Medal of Honour.

Private Joe Mann CMH

As Lieutenant Wierzbowski's platoon finally rejoined 3/502 PIR, having been feared lost for the last two days, word spread of an event that had happened in the forest

Earlier on Tuesday 19th September Lieutenant Wierzbowski's platoon was still isolated in the woods near the bridge. In the morning mist, German infantry had reached a point within grenade range of the small group of Americans.

'Sergeant Betras threw a grenade, and then several others threw. But the Germans had beaten them to the throw and grenades were already on their way to the foxholes. Two hit the top of the embankment.'

These were thrown back but another exploded on Engineer Private Laino's machine gun.

'It blew his left eye out, blinded the other eye and made a pulp of his face ... Another grenade came over ... hit Laino on the knee and bounced off into his foxhole. Laino, still blinded, reached down groping for it, found it and tossed it from his foxhole just a split second before it exploded.'

For this coolness in action, Private Laino earned the Silver Star.

The final grenade again fell in the large trench containing six wounded paratroopers, that included Private First Class Mann,

Joe Mann, CMH.

whose wounded arms were bound up. He felt the grenade land behind him and yelled 'Grenade' and

'fully conscious of what he was doing he lay back and took the explosion with his own back'.

Private Mann whispered to Lieutenant Wierzbowiski, 'My back's gone'. Without a further sound, he died a few minutes later; 'the bravest man his comrades had ever known.' Surrounded and outnumbered the Americans surrendered but were released later that afternoon. Private First Class Joe Mann was awarded a posthumous Congressional Medal of Honor. An excerpt from his citation reads:

'His outstanding gallantry and his magnificent conduct were an everlasting inspiration to his comrades for whom he gave his life.'

Retrace the route back to the **N620**. Turn **left** towards **Best**; on the right is the **The Wings of Liberation Museum** (Bevrijdende Veleugels). This is an enthusiast's museum. The museum is rapidly improving in both content and presentation and is well worth a visit. Its central theme is the liberation by 101st Airborne Division but covers a number of other areas as well. In addition to Second World War vehicles and equipment, much of the military hardware dates from the post 1945 period.

In the main building is a general display that gives a broad view of the War and has a very good audio-visual presentation on MARKET GARDEN and the complicated series of actions fought by 101st Airborne. Other halls (formerly stores and garages), cover the part played by the 101st in MARKET GARDEN. Mannequins portray the men, equipment and vehicles in realistic settings along with Dutch civilians. Also covered is the liberation of Best by 51st (Highland) Division (XII Corps) who took the town a month later. Other halls contain American vehicles and equipment and aircraft, including a comprehensive section on Hitler's V weapons that were launched from the Netherlands. A C-47 Skytrain or Dakota has pride of place near the entrance.

Up to date opening time and entry charges can be found on the Museum's web site at http://www.wiingsofliberation.nl

CHAPTER SEVEN

ST OEDENRODE
The misdrop, capture and defence of the town

From the Wings of Liberation Museum' Car Park **turn right**. On to the N620 towards Best. In three-quarters of a mile, turn right onto **Molenheideweg**. This road takes the visitor along the southern edge of the Son DZs. After a mile and a half, turn left onto **Brouwerskampweg** and drive on across DZ C onto LZ W. In the late summer, before the harvest, the tall maize (or corn) can make it difficult to appreciate how open this large DZ area is. At a crossroads turn right onto **Hoogstraat** and follow it across DZ B / LZ W. **Turn left at the T-junction** go across the roundabout / junction towards **St Oedenrode. Do not go onto the main road north.**
Follow the road through the **centre of St Oedenrode** (good shops, cafes and bars) and across the Old River Dommel Bridge. **Go straight across the roundabout.**

While 2nd and 3rd 502 PIR were being sucked into the battle at Best, the Regiment's 1st Battalion advanced to St Oedenrode to the north of DZ B. In common with 101st Airborne's other units, the Battalion's objectives were bridges. In this case, over the River Dommel, which, though not large, meandered through a shallow but boggy valley that was, consequently, an obstacle to tanks.

The Battalion had assembled at a crossroads to the north-east of the DZ. Lieutenant Colonel Cassidy's plan was for Company C, followed by Battalion Headquarters, to advance and secure the town's two road bridges. Meanwhile, two Company B platoons were to secure a footbridge at the eastern end of the town. Company B's third platoon, guided by the Dutch underground, went to investigate reports of enemy in Nijnsel. Company A was to follow Battalion HQ as a reserve.

As Company C advanced, they came under small arms fire and were soon halted. However, the well-trained paratroopers, supported by the battalion's mortars, soon manoeuvred into positions from which they were able, in the ensuing fire fight, to overwhelm the rear echelon Germans. The paratroopers continued their advance and came across, what would have been a, potentially, far more dangerous opposition. Two

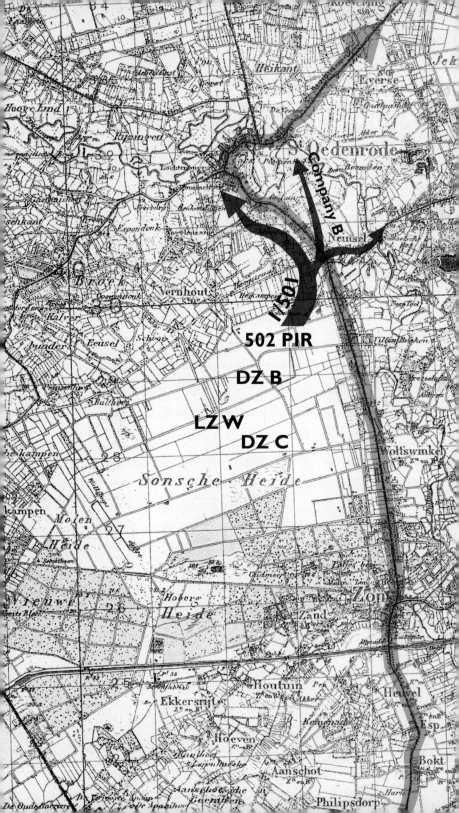

Heikant

Everse

St Oedenrode

Company B

Eeusel

1/501

502 PIR

DZ B

LZW

DZ C

Sonsche Heide

Wolfswinkel

Molen Heide

Hooge Lind

Brock

Vernhout

Kalver

bunders

Schoor

de kampen

kampen

Vreuwel De Heide

Hoberg

Zand

Zon

Houtum

Heuvel

Ekkersrijt

Hoeven

Aanschot

Philipsdorp

Bokt

German Mark IV tanks lay knocked out on the road. These tanks had been victims of the P-51s and Spitfires that had been providing top cover to the drop, who on spotting the tanks had dived on their prey well ahead of the advancing paratroopers. The leading tank blocked the road but with its engine still running and the commander's body hanging out of the hatch. The paratroopers decided to remove the body and drive the tank off the road.

'Stackhouse was up on the tank with someone trying to help him pull the German out. Whatever the foot of the dead German touched or hit, it caused an explosion. Private Stackhouse was blown off the tank by the blast, which drove his barber's tools through the pockets of his jacket and they protruded through his body. He was dead.'

Opposition stiffened again and Company C suffered further casualties, as the paratroopers moved into the town. However, there were no significant guards on the bridges and Private First Class Marohn recalls how:

'As we came up to the village, the shooting started and things began to get hot. I was told to check out a large house. I went through it thoroughly from top to bottom ... When I came out, the platoon had continued to move into the village and I was alone. I was going up Main Street when Sergeant Kochenour came out of an alley through the side door of a building. He asked me if I was thirsty, naturally. I said yes. ... It was a small Dutch pub. Ken went behind the bar and drew us each a large glass of beer. It really hit the spot. We could hear the machine guns down the street. The war was still on. We finished the beer and then continued to the street.'

As in many other cases, the fight for a town was promptly joined by Dutch Underground fighters, whose numbers were greatly swelled by any brave Dutchman who could get hold of a captured weapon. However, they mainly were most useful as guides and for gathering information on where the Germans were hiding or fighting in the town. Private Marohn continued:

'We went in and several Dutch people who were there led us to the kitchen and pointed to a door. It led to a cellar. Three German NCOs had taken refuge there. They came up at our invitation and we relieved them of their pistols. They were from a finance unit and were the next day to pay the troops in the area.'

St Oedenrode from the east. Site of what was thought to be a footbridge is now a major road, by-passing the town.

Another feature of the fighting, common to many other points on Hell's Highway, was the contrast between the exuberant welcome of the Dutch people and the serious business of fighting. Local priest Father Arnold de Groot has recorded his first encounter with his liberators:

> *'It was a little after 17.00 hours. On the cellar grating, we heard footsteps and a voice speaking over a radio. I said, "I just heard English being spoken!" Nobody believed me. We saw them all over the market square ... We all stormed outside and stammered our English welcome and soon the market square was filled with townspeople. The Burgomeister got back his chain of office and he was congratulated and we all danced around him. German prisoners were being brought to the town hall, where the leader of the guards was a civilian. He told us, "It isn't over yet!" Shortly afterwards, the shooting started again.'*

The town was eventually secured by 20.00 hours, after a number of running engagements, which damaged parts of the town including the monastery.

On the eastern approaches to the town, Company B found that the footbridge had been replaced by a new road bridge. This is clearly shown as such on the air photographs taken in early September 1944 but it was still marked as a footbridge on the planners' maps. Crossing the Bridge Company B took up positions blocking the road in the eastern part of the town.

At the end of the day, another young priest, Father Herman Peeters, was able to celebrate St Oedenrode's liberation in style:

> *'... there was a German jeep which had been captured. It contained many bottles of brandy and boxes of cigars. I hadn't eaten. The Americans gave us priests two bottles of brandy so we could celebrate. I became very sick because I drank brandy on an empty stomach. I was one of many who were very sick that night!'*

126

Monday 18 September 1944

Early on D+1, a force of enemy infantry attacked St Oedenrode from the south-west. These were probably from the *Fallschirmjäger* Battalion Ewald of the s'Hertogenbosch Training and Replacement Regiment. As there was a four mile gap between 502 PIR at Best and St Oedenrode, the young German paratroopers were able to slip through and, as far as 1/502 PIR were concerned, attack them from behind. However, Company A 1/502 PIR counter attacked. Lacking superior numbers, the partly trained German *Fallschirmjäger* were no match for the experienced Americans, who overran an enemy mortar position and took a number of prisoners.

An incident on 18 September indicated that, while the situation was relatively quiet in St Oedenrode, the Germans were present in considerable numbers to the north of the town. An error was made by a group of staff officers from Headquarters 1st Allied Airborne Army driving north with their escort, along with two Jeep loads of paratroopers from the Divisional Reconnaissance Platoon. Private First Class Flanagan of Company C, 1/502 PIR recalls:

'... a convoy of Jeeps came through our road block. The private on the roadblock told the Army Air Corps [Air Force] *major that the Germans were up the road towards Schijndel. The major said he could read a map and proceeded to go up the road.'*

The convoy of seven Jeeps had taken the road to Schijndel rather than following Hell's Highway towards Veghel. They had barely gone a mile when the leading vehicle bumped the enemy. Private First Class Wysocki was an escort in the second vehicle:

'As we approached a road and made our turn, there was a German machine gunner at a roadblock. He fired a burst at us and we opened up on him. There was another gunner on the other side of the road. We couldn't stop so we proceeded on ahead to get out of the range of the machine guns. As we did this, we

The old bridge over the Dommel in the centre of St Oedenrode.

came into this little town. To our surprise, it was filled with Germans. The road led to a circular roundabout so we went to the right and hoped to circle around and come right back. We thought we were part of a western the way we were going through and shooting up the town – loaded as it was with Germans.'

The 1st Airborne Army Colonel's Jeep managed to escape and summoned help. The remaining Jeeps were driven off the roads by fire and the paratroopers took to the drainage ditches for cover. Two squads of 2nd Platoon, Company C were dispatched from St Oedenrode to rescue the Jeep crews. Private Flanagan was with the leading group:

'... An MG-42 cut loose. I let them have a full clip of M-1 ball – and I ducked down into the ditch just in time as another MG-42 mowed the bushes that I had been behind. ... About this time, I heard the pum - pum - pump of someone stuffing a mortar in an expert manner. I had previously learned to pay attention to little things like that. The first hit about 100 yards to my left. Number two about 75 yards ... Number four hit about 25 yards away and I knew that the next one was going to be so close so I coiled up in a ball on the side of the ditch. I didn't hear it explode. I was booted up the slope and into the air several feet. Everything in slow motion until I started down and I bounced when I hit the asphalt.'

Despite the enemy fire, 2nd Platoon were able to put down sufficient covering fire of their own to enable several jeep loads remount their vehicles and make it back to their own lines. The remainder, mostly wounded, were taken prisoner. However, the proximity of so many Germans so close to the route north, was a worrying development.

The Road to Schijndel – Tuesday 19 September 1944

Elation following the arrival of the Guards Armoured Division in St Oedenrode, bedecked with orange flags and bunting, was tempered by word from the Underground that 1/502 should expect an attack from the direction of Schijnel. Lieutenant Larson's platoon was promptly dispatched as a fighting patrol up the road. They forced back the German outpost line with fire, but were soon halted by what was assessed to be a reinforced infantry company. Taking cover in the ditches, the Americans were unable to win a second firefight and another Company C platoon, from under Lieutenant Mewborn, was dispatched to help extricate the patrol. However, the Germans pressed forward and, making the most of their numerical advantage, attempted to outflank the withdrawing Americans. Again the battle escalated and as the 101st's historian described, '... all of Company C was drawn into the fight'. The history continues:

> 'Watching from his battalion CP, Colonel Cassidy saw that the company was hard pressed ... Suddenly he remembered a tank that had come limping into the town that morning with the Irish Guards column. Unable to go more than five miles an hour it had dropped out of the line and stopped in front of the battalion CP.'

The Sherman was left with only its commander and driver; the gunner, loader and radio operator having accompanied the Irish Guard's main body north. Awaiting repair, Lance Sergeant James (Paddy) McCrory, responded to an appeal for help; 'Hell, yes!' but missing vital crew, he was going to need help. Taking the gunner's seat with its extremely limited vision, Paddy McCrory needed help spotting the enemy. Sergeant Nickrent and Private O'Brien, both from Headquarters 1/502, stepped forward and the tank roared forward into action – at little more than walking pace.

As the tank left the village, the volume of small arms fire helped Sergeant Nickrent overcome his natural paratroopers' suspicion of tanks. They spotted three vehicle-mounting quad 20mm guns engaging Company C from the flank. Approaching unseen, Sergeant McCrory slithered down into the gunner's seat and, eye pressed against the rubber sight, laid his gun on the nearest enemy vehicle. At 150 yards, the first 20mm was reduced to scrap and the other two were dispatched in quick succession. With these three 'kills', Paddy McCrory proved himself to be an accomplished armoured soldier by both loading and accurately laying his 75mm gun. As the 101st recorded,

> 'The timing could not have been more opportune. It came just as C's whole line was getting its heaviest deluge of 88, 20 mm and mortar fire in the middle of an enemy assault. The destruction of the enemy battery stifled the enemy offensive and for a few minutes, the action remained in the balance.
> McCrory went on up the road towards Schijndel. Sergeant

Nickrent, again on the outside, saw what looked like another camouflaged gun position and he yelled until he got McCrory's attention. McCrory searched for about ten seconds, then cut loose and destroyed the gun with two rounds. The tank limped on.'

An ammunition truck was McCrory's next victim; his shot initiating 'a most satisfactory pyrotechnic display'. However, the fire was getting too heavy and Sergeant Nickrent was forced off the turret and took cover behind the Sherman's bulk. Eventually he was forced to take cover in a ditch, joining three Germans who promptly surrendered. Other Germans, equally keen to surrender soon joined them. As the Sherman made its stately progress towards Schijndel, Private O'Brien, realising that his Sergeant had a problem to deal with, scrambled onto the advancing tank. Taking Paddy McCrory's Sten gun, he fired bursts into other Germans occupying the roadside ditches. Together with 'its tank' Company C drove the enemy back 500 metres. The gain was consolidated, when a troop of Guards' tanks arrived. However, as an experienced soldier, mindful of General Taylor's instructions, Lieutenant Colonel Cassidy was not about to loose the advantage, by becoming embroiled in a close quarter battle with a strong German force. Fifty-three prisoners were taken and thirty German bodies were recovered form the battlefield.

Back in St Oedenrode, The two Irish Guardsmen were warmly thanked and invited to be honorary members of 1/502 PIR. In a memorable phrase, Sergeant Paddy McCrory provided the battalion with an unofficial motto, 'When in doubt, lash out'. Paddy McCrory and his forgotten driver, were soldiers who would earn the respect and affection of fellow fighting men the world over.

Leaving **St Oedenrode** take the **N265** north towards **Veghel, Uden** and **Nijmegen**. Pass through the hamlet of **Koevering**, to which we will return at the appropriate point in the tour.

CHAPTER EIGHT

VEGHEL
The misdrop, capture and defence of the town

One of the first things that members of 501 PIR ('The Geronimos') learnt as they tried to orientate themselves on their DZs, with the help of Dutch civilians, was that Veghel was pronounced as Feghel. Although Veghel was the furthest of 101st Airborne's objectives from XXX Corps start-line in the Neerpelt bridgehead, it was of particular importance. 501 PIR were to seize bridges across a double water feature with the town of Veghel as the 'meat in the sandwich'. Should the enemy hold a single crossing and the town, the paratroopers would have considerable difficulty in opening the route north to Nijmegen and Arnhem.

'The mission ... was to secure the four rail and highway bridges over the Aa River and the Zuid Willems Vart Canal. According to the original plan, the whole Regiment was to be dropped on DZ A, south west of both these waterways.'

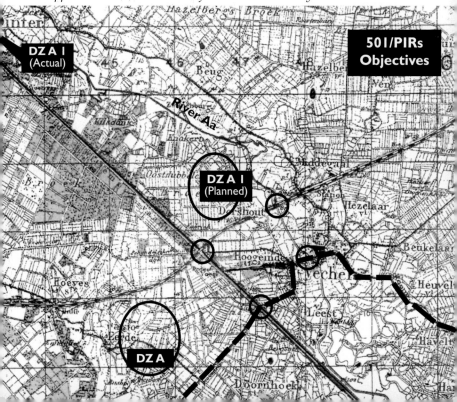

However, during the planning process Lieutenant Colonel Kinnard stressed that it would be a considerable advantage if he could have dropped a battalion between the Canal and his second objectives on the River Aa. A delay in taking the Canal bridges would give the Germans time to man defences or blow the bridges. The airforces, without any flak to consider, were happy to drop 1/501 PIR's serials on DZ A1. In his briefings, Colonel Kinnard allocated the railway bridge over the canal to Company A, Company C were to take the rail bridge across the Aa, while Company B had furthest to go to the road bridge across the river. However, he stressed that his troopers, less a platoon from each company allocated to specific bridges, should head to the nearest bridge. Jumping with 2 and 3/501 PIR on DZ A were two platoons of 326 Engineers. In addition to disarming any demolition charges on the bridges, they were to build an extra bridge alongside the single-track Canal Bridge, thus eliminating a choke point on XXX Corp's route north.

It was not planned that 501 PIR would have to fight on its own for long. XXX Corps's Operation Order saw reinforcements arriving close on the heels of Guards Armoured Division as early as midday on 18 September:

'A Regimental Group of 8 Armd Bde will advance to area VEGHEL and there come under operational command of 501 RCT, with a view to helping to clear 30 Corps' main axis of advance into VEGHEL area.'

A road sign, originally from Veghel, now at the Son Museum.

ST.-OEDENRODE 9	UDEN	9
SON 16	GRAVE	26
EINDHOVEN 27	NIJMEGEN	54

In the event, they did not arrive until 19 September, as a result of the delay in breaking out and the blowing of the Son Bridge. However, even with these delays, XXX Corps' Movement Order put other conditions that would cause further delay to the advancing troops:

'35 VTM [vehicles to the mile] *at 10 MPH. There will be NO movement on the main axis during the hours of darkness. ... Groups leaguring for the night*

132

will probably have to do so on the main road owing to the nature of the ground. No lights will be allowed on the main axis or in its immediate vicinity. Rearward traffic on the main axis of advance will be kept to the barest minimum for at least the first 48 hours.'

Clearly, the vulnerability of unsupported airborne troops had not been made plain to XXX Corps. It should have been stressed that vehicles using lights on a narrow corridor had to be accepted to keep to time. The blame for this lack of coordination must stop at the respective army commanders not at the lower levels. However, as the overall MARKET GARDEN situation deteriorated, the XXX Corps ban on night movement was generally ignored.

DZ A, used by 2 and 3/501 PIR, is located in the fields to the left of the **N265**, north of **Koevering** and south east of **Eerde** before reaching **Veghel**.

Drop Zone A – Sunday 17 September 1944

On Sunday 17 September 1944, 2 and 3/501st were the leading elements of 101st Airborne Division, starting their drop at 13.06 hours, on DZ A, which was well marked by the Regiment's pathfinders. The two battalions successfully dropped in tight groups. Corporal Beyer described the landing.

'Landing unopposed. Terrain flat and sandy with frequent patches of pine trees. Civilians much in evidence, cordial. Dropped about one mile west of designated DZ Light injuries sustained on jump.'

Led by Company D, 2/501 had secured the Willemsuaart Canal Road Bridge by 14.30 hours and 3/501 PIR captured the Railway Bridge. The official accounts describe the initial stages of operation as 'unopposed'. However, Private Cartledge recalled that a German motorcyclist appeared on the road bridge and how,

'The fool had stopped and jumped off his motorbike with his machine pistol and was going to win the battle of the bridge by himself.'

In addition to the motorcyclist, several German vehicles were shot up or captured. Behind the battalions' advance, a roadblock was established on the Veghel – St Oedenrode road and Eerde was occupied by elements of 3/501 PIR. Corporal Flanagan

recorded how, having been dispatched to the roadblock, he found:

'... two GIs in a foxhole beside the road with a bazooka and they yelled, "Get off the road there's a tank coming!" ... "It's OK, it's a Limey tank!" ... wearing American uniform, I walked out on the highway and sure enough this tank came barrelling down the highway towards me - a medium tank.'

This tank was probably a part of the same troop that had two Mark IVs knocked-out by Allied fighter bombers on the outskirts of St Oedenrode, some two miles south. Corporal Flanagan continued:

'The tank commander was standing up in the turret and waving his hand. I immediately started to think, what word should I greet him with but I am listening to a little voice in my mind - that's a funny colour for a Limey tank. They paint theirs OD, like ours and about that time, I realized I was looking at the black German cross painted on the front. The guy who waved at me had a Luger in his hand ... I had my M1 rifle under my right arm and I crouched in the middle of the road and brought it up like a Kentucky squirrel hunter trying to snap off a shot before he did. He shot first and I heard the snap of his round past my left ear. I shot from the hip and he threw up his hands and went down the turret. To this day I don't know if I shot him through the navel or missed him by ten yards.'

The tank thundered by towards the bridge, with the paratroopers at the roadblock attempting to engage the tank but surprised by its arrival of the tank, the bazooka man failed to arm the warhead. A common enough problem, even with some twenty-first Century anti-tank weapons! At the bridge, HQ 501 PIR also made a mistake in identifying the tank. Colonel Johnson and his staff were engaged by machine-gun fire and:

'... ended up dangling from the bridge supports while the tank roared across the town. It went clear down the twisting street, came out in the main section of the town where priests were passing out

An American bazooka, 2.36 calibre.

134

beer and pretzels and people were dancing in the street and made
a right turn, being pursued by a pathfinder sergeant who was
[forlornly] shooting a .45 pistol into the motor in an attempt to
disable it'.

The tank made good its escape.

Drop Zone A1 – Sunday 17 September 1944

Heading for DZ A1, 1/501 PIR, who had been loaded aboard the first forty aircraft of the stream, lost their pathfinder's to anti-aircraft fire as they crossed the coast into Belgium. Sergeant George Koskimaki recorded that as they diverged from the main body towards DZ A1:

'The lead plane had to depend on the skill of it's pilot and
navigator to determine the locations of the fields in which to drop
the 600-man battalion. They missed!'

As Colonel Kinnard left the door of his C-47 at 13.01 hours, he immediately realized that 'It's the wrong field again'. Neither of his key landmarks of Veghel and the railway line were in sight, as he descended the seven-hundred feet beneath his white silk canopy. Unable to identify their position on landing, Private Batts of the Battalion's Intelligence Section was dispatched to find out where they were. The answer was that they were around the village of Kameren, some three and a half miles north west of their intended DZ.

The battalion had been dropped in a tight pattern and with the orange smoke grenades and the red battalion ID flags being waved, the battalion was quickly assembled and ready to move off. However, there were the usual jump casualties, some of whom could be made mobile. Staff Sergeant White recalled,

'I hurt my ankle very bad on the jump but I hobbled around
fairly well. On the march from the DZ to Veghel, a Dutch family
gave me a bicycle to ride'.

However, eight men were sufficiently badly injured as to be unable to be moved because the battalion had no transport. They were left behind, with the doctor, in Heeswijk Castle that lay on the eastern end of their DZ, guarded by a group of Headquarter Company soldiers under command of Captain Burd. Once the fractures were sorted out, the group was to find transport to take them to Veghel but comfortable in their castle, assisted by a friendly population there seemed to be no hurry.

With commendable speed, 1/501 PIR moved the three and a

half miles to Veghel, with many of the leading paratroopers running, heavily laden, down the road. As they entered Veghel they met 2/501 PIR coming from the opposite direction, and together they cleared the town and took fifty prisoners. However, taking up defensive positions was delayed by an enthusiastic welcome from the Dutch population. The slow organization of Veghel's defence was to be the root cause of problems later.

For 1/501 PIR the day was spoilt by news that, shortly after they had left their wounded in the care of Headquarter Company in Castle Heeswijk, Germans had arrived and 'unexpectedly attacked the group, forcing it to retreat to a large stone building'. These were the leading elements of a 'March' battalion arriving from s'Hertogenbosch. According to the divisional history, Colonel Kinnard:

> '... at once asked for permission to send a company in relief. The Regimental CO, Colonel Johnson, did not feel that a company could be spared from the mission; the defence of Veghel, and would agree to nothing larger than a platoon.'

The platoon was duly dispatched under Lieutenant Rafferty but he was stopped eight hundred yards short of the ancient castle outside Heeswijk by German fire and forced to dig-in.

Castle Heeswijk located near DZ A1.

The town of Veghel has expanded greatly in the last fifty years, but the four bridges are still standing, all be it, modernized. Having crossed the Willemsvaart Canal take the sliproad on to the **N279**. **Turn left** and go under the main road. **Turn left again at the traffic lights**. Follow the road down to the canal bank road. The road and rail bridges are to the left and right respectively.

The Defence of Veghel – Night Sunday 17/Monday 18 September 1944

At last light, 1/501 PIR was holding the two Aa Bridges, 2/501 PIR the canal bridges and 3/501 PIR was concentrated around Eerde. In common with the remainder of the Screaming Eagles, 501 PIR did not have its artillery battalion on 17 September, only it's 81mm mortars, with limited ammunition. General Taylor was forced by the need to cover his very large area, to bring in 146 jeeps along with his 6,641 paratroops, at the expense of heavy support weapons. Nowhere was the effect of this felt more keenly than at Veghel.

One constant feature of the North West European Campaign was the German's ability to mount prompt and dangerous counter-attacks. By midnight, Jungwirth's *Fallschirmjaeger* Training Replacement Regiment was arriving from s'Hertogenbosch. However, only after a series of attacks, did the Americans fully appreciate the enemy's strength.

In the north-west sector of Veghel, Company E had been unable to properly co-ordinate its positions and register its mortar defensive fire tasks before dark. In the early autumn mist that settled in the valley of the Aa, the Germans mounted a silent attack at 02.00 hours. Approximately 300 *Fallschirmjäger*, advancing astride the canal, drove in Company E's outposts around the large warehouse building on the canal bank three hundred meters to the west, after a sharp fight. Just to the left were the outposts of Company D. Private Cavaluzzo recalls:

> *'I was on outpost duty ... Company E was engaged in close-in fighting to our right. This had us sweating because we feared getting cut off from our MLR* [Main Line of Resistance]. *It actually sounded as though the Krauts had gotten behind us.'*

However, the German attack was solely along the line of the canal and the outposts fell back on the MLR to the west of the Railway Bridge, where Lieutenant MacGregor's platoon was dug-in. The citation for his posthumous Silver Star reads:

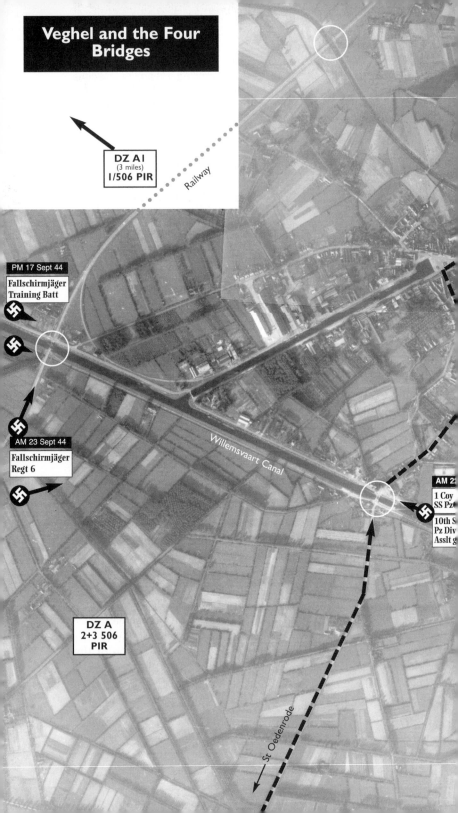

Veghel and the Four Bridges

DZ A1
(3 miles)
1/506 PIR

Railway

PM 17 Sept 44

Fallschirmjäger Training Batt

AM 23 Sept 44

Fallschirmjäger Regt 6

Willemsvaart Canal

AM 2:
1 Coy SS Pz
10th S Pz Div Asslt g

DZ A
2+3 506 PIR

St Oedenrode

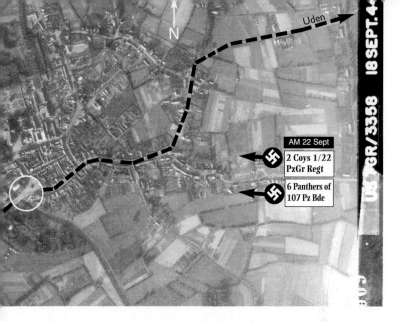

'... *the overwhelming superiority of the enemy greatly taxed the strength of his platoon and Lt MacGregor was ordered to withdraw his men. Realizing that a critical situation had developed and that rapid withdrawal was imperative, Lt MacGregor remained at the centre of the road junction fully exposed to enemy fire, and directed the movement of his confused forces. Desperately shouting orders to his men, he held back the onrushing enemy by firing his sub-machine gun from his exposed position, killing several of the enemy. This afforded his men sufficient time to effect an orderly withdrawal. Although seriously wounded, he remained to direct his troops until the position was overrun and he became, temporarily, a prisoner. He was rescued the following day by counter-attacking, friendly forces ...*'

Lieutenant MacGregor died of his wounds.

The initial attack was beaten off and the Rail Bridge re-captured but, during the course of the night, two more major and several minor attacks on other parts of the western perimeter were mounted by the Germans. Pressure was considerable and Company E, who bore the brunt of the fighting lost seven killed and twenty-six wounded before further counter-attacks finally drove the Germans back at dawn. 3/501 PIR at Eerde, was also attacked. Pastor (Padre) Willi Schiffer who was accompanying the young *Fallschirmjäger* from a battalion of Jungwirth Training Replacement Regiment and recorded:

'The heavy-weapons companies were held back, while the light infantry companies walked straight into the machine gun fire of the Americans who were hiding in the station. In a bitter man to man fight, the Americans were driven away and went on along the railway track. Supported by flak guns brought up from s'Hertogenbosch, we finally collected enough troops to attack the railway bridge in front of Veghel, which we took in the afternoon. Shortly afterwards, to our complete consternation, we received orders to withdraw! What had happened? The Battalion HQ and HQ Company, which had remained in Schijndel, had been attacked by armoured cars [2/HCR], operating singly, from the direction of St Oedenrode, and they were afraid that an attack would follow into our flank. Their fears were groundless, as it was several days before larger units could be brought forward by both sides, and the real battle began. But the very next day a Regiment of our 59th Infantry Division had to retrace our path and were wiped out.'

However, the strength of Jungwirth's attack on Veghel was to cause Colonel Johnson to withdraw 3/501 PIR from Eerde to hold his vital ground around the Veghel bridges. The remainder of 18 September was taken up with consolidating positions and patrolling.

The Heeswijk/Dinther Manoeuvre – Wednesday 20 September 1944

Return to the N265. Head north. At the next major traffic light junction **turn left** onto **Wilgensraat** following signs to **Heeswijk – Dinther**. Leaving Veghel the area of the American attack on 20 September is to the left.

The 101st's divisional history reminds readers that:

'The mission ... was not to kill Germans but to create and hold the corridor. Aggressive patrolling was taken for granted, but if too many groups spent too much time roaming around the country looking for a fight, the resulting engagements might seriously weaken the ability of the Division to accomplish its original mission. On the other hand, the road couldn't be defended by sitting on it and letting the enemy organize his

The Heeswijk-Dinther Manoeuvre

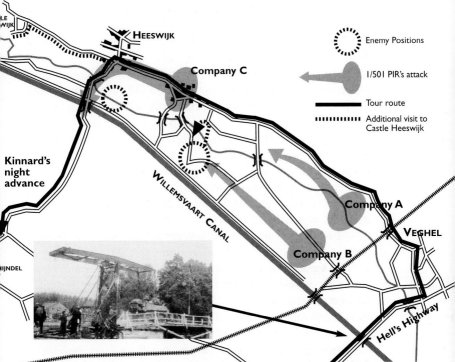

HEESWIJK	Enemy Positions
Company C	1/501 PIR's attack
	Tour route
Kinnard's night advance	Additional visit to Castle Heeswijk
WILLEMSVAART CANAL	Company A
	VEGHEL
DIJNDEL	Company B
	Hell's Highway

strength for an overwhelming attack at one crucial spot.'

On the morning of D+3 Colonel Johnson had sufficient information to be sure that one of *Kampfgruppe* Jungwirth's march battalions was in an isolated position to his west; in a position where he could eliminate them as a threat. Consequently, he committed Lieutenant Colonel Kinnard's 1st Battalion to a daring operation but it was over familiar ground towards the Battalion's unintended DZ beyond Heeswijk. The mission was the destruction of enemy forces north of the Canal, rather than the capture or holding of ground.

Colonel Kinnard's plan was to encircle the enemy. Company C had already established the bulk of its strength in Dinter where it manned the Regiment's western outposts. They were to advance to Heeswijk, outflanking the enemy and taking up cut-off positions to his rear. Company A, astride the Aa, and Company B on the left, immediately north of the Canal, were to drive the enemy west towards Company C's position. The Canal was an obstacle to all manoeuvre, while the Aa could be

141

forded by infantry at most points on its length and, once contained between the two forces and the Canal, the German battalion would be destroyed. H Hour for the attack was 09.30 hours.

Company C pushing west from Dinther, well ahead of Companies A and B, was soon in action. They brushed aside limited opposition and reaching Heeswijk, as Private Carpenter recorded:

'... we swung left from the Dinther – Heeswijk intersection, we ran into enemy fire and had to fight our way to the canal. Captain Phillips was leading us. The platoons were well deployed. We pushed our way through whatever Germans were in front of us to a drawbridge at the canal and anchored ourselves in position.'

Radio operator Private Haller, accompanying Captain Phillips described the action at the canal bridge:

'I remember down by the canal, the Germans raised a white flag. They wanted to give up. They had me, because I could speak German, and one other fellow, who was to cover me, go down to there to talk to the Germans. They opened fire on us. We jumped into the canal. I yelled to Captain Phillips to "Let them have it!" Our men opened fire again for about half an hour and the Germans gave up. We got about fifty prisoners. A lot were real young and some very old fellows. They weren't good soldiers and the young ones didn't even shave yet.'

Thus, the American cut-offs were in position and they had eliminated a German position in depth.

Meanwhile, as Company C moved out, Companies A and B were beginning their sweep along the relatively narrow but shallow Aa Valley. Tanks would not have fared well in the country bisected by drainage ditches, even if they had been available. However, helped by brave Dutchmen who pointed out German positions, the advance went relatively well. Such information provided by Hans Kropman. He:

'... pinpointed their position on the map. That made it possible for Lieutenant Puhalski and his 3rd Platoon to cross the canal on the southern flank, move north to capture two hundred men with a group of 45 men.'

However, not all gave up so easily. Coming under machine gun fire from a windmill, Companies A and B engaged the Germans in a fire fight, with small arms and mortars. Under cover of this

The modern bridge across the Willemsaart Canal at Veghel.

The railway bridge, now a foot bridge, was held by Company E, 2/501 PIR.

The site of Heeswijk Canal Bridge.

fire, they closed in on the enemy outposts, using fire and manoeuvre across the open fields or used drainage ditches as covered approaches. A platoon from Company B knocked out three multiple 20mm anti-aircraft guns that were causing casualties, having noticed that the guns were not dug in and hence vulnerable to small arms fire. This denied the *Fallschirmjäger* crucial fire support, while Lieutenant Puhalski's manoeuvre to the rear undermined their morale, which was already fragile, having suffered heavy casualties in the previous days. As noted above, this situation prompted at least a company of German's from a training battalion to surrender. The key moment was when Lieutenant Turner appeared, standing confidently in the open, appealing for the *Fallschirmjäger* to surrender but when he tried to approach, he was shot dead. Another casualty was Lieutenant Puhalski who, as Sergeant West recalled, was killed when:

> '... the Germans put up a white flag and then shot him when he stood up'.

Lieutenant Blackmon, referring to this incident said,

> 'This taught us a lot. We didn't worry about white flags anymore. If a man stood up, we would honor him. We didn't pay any attention to flags.'

Tactically, this first phase of the operation was a considerable success. Rather than pressing home a direct attack on the main German position, the Americans had outmanoeuvred an enemy force in well-prepared positions that were supported by numerous machine guns. Those Germans who had not surrendered were driven west towards Company C's cut-offs. According to the 101st's history:

> 'When the two Companies moved forward again it was shoulder to shoulder, for the sector had narrowed. Advance was quick for the back of the resistance had been broken. By 15.00 hours, the two companies abreast were only five hundred yards short of Dinther. Patrols were out along the highway to round up any enemy who tried to escape to the north-east.'

The Germans withdrew into *ad hoc* positions, which they occupied in the narrow neck of land between the Aa and the canal. Here they stopped and realizing that they were almost cut off, some made a break to the north but were turned back by fire from Company C in Heeswijk. The divisional historian describes the action:

'It was about 15.00 that the Germans made their all-out attempt to break out of the trap. With a rush, they moved towards a wooded area along the canal. But Captain Phillips had carefully placed a machine gun to cover their route. It caught them in the flank, mowed some of them down, and drove others back.'

By 17.30 hours, it was all over, 418 Germans were taken prisoner, along with approximately forty dead and a similar number of wounded. Lieutenant Colonel Kinnard had achieved his aim and destroyed an enemy battalion and eliminated a significant threat to Hell's Highway. The day ended with Company C occupying a bridgehead south of the canal, while B occupied a perimeter around Heeswijk and A around Dinther.

Old men and boys are among this batch of *Wehrmacht* prisoners.

Drive on into **Dinther** and on to the **Heeswijk** end of the village. To reach **Castle Heeswijk** and DZ A1 from the church at the centre of Heeswijk village, follow the signs to **Berlirum** and **s'Hertogensosch**. 1/501 PIR's misdrop took place in the open fields beyond village. Keep an eye out for the **left turn to Castle Heeswijk**. To reach the Canal Bridge from the centre of **Heeswijk village** take the turn opposite the church signed towards **Schijndel**. The first bridge crosses the River Aa. Four hundred yards further on is the Canal. A platoon taking up positions along this road cut off the Germans. Follow the sign to **Schijndel** across the new bridge.

CHAPTER NINE

SCHIJNDEL
The big trap that was not to be

The Situation and Plans

By the evening of 21 September 1944, Hells Highway, north of the Bailey Bridge built by the Royal Engineers at Son, had been open to Guards Armoured Division traffic for sixty hours. However, the attacks by 107 Panzer Brigade had twice closed the route and German bombing of Eindhoven had severely disrupted the vital logistic traffic. In the previous four days, the resource starved British VIII and XII Corps had advanced sufficiently far, to release 506 PIR from defending Eindhoven, for tasks further up Hell's Highway. Also in 101st Airborne's area, the battle at Best had reached its climax the day before and beyond Veghel, the Guards had reached Grave and the 82nd Airborne Division. On 19 and 20 September, the Guardsmen joined the 82nd's paratroopers in fighting a bitter battle for the bridges across the River Waal. Meanwhile, Korps Feldt was attacking the 82nd's positions south of Nijmegen, from the Reichswald and exerting so much pressure, that when the Waal Bridges were finally taken, the Allies had insufficient resources available to force the last ten miles to Arnhem. XXX Corps, who

The church tower at Schijndel was used as an artillery OP but early morning mist on 22 September meant that the observer could not see the enemy.

now had the American airborne divisions under command, had only the sketchiest idea of what was going on in Arnhem. However, already forty-eight hours behind schedule, XXX Corps realized that 1st Airborne Division must be under severe pressure. MARKET GARDEN was not going well but the Allies and 101st Airborne in particular were far from defeated.

On Thursday 21 September, *Feldmarschall* Model issued orders for concerted attacks on the Allied Corridor that now reached fifty miles into the rear area. With growing numbers of troops, who had escaped the Allied trap on the Channel Coast, now arriving, he believed that he could cut-off and destroy the four Allied divisions now fighting in the Nijmegen / Arnhem area. In contrast to the Allied view of the battle, the Germans were optimistic that they could administer a bloody check on Montgomery.

An entry in LXXXVIII Korps war diary summarizes the orders given to *Generaloberst* Student's First *Fallchirmjäger* Army:

> *'Feldmarschall Model has ordered that the enemy columns marching on Nijmegen are to be attacked at the Veghel bottleneck on 22 September from the west and east. This is to be helped by a panzer brigade from Heeresgruppe B from the east and through a Kampfgruppe of the 59th Division from the west, consisting of two battalions strongly supported by artillery and Panzerjäger* [assault guns].'

With the towns of St Oedenrode and Veghel secured by 502 and 501 PIR respectively, 101st Airborne was mounting a mobile defence of the Corridor. Their aim was to keep the enemy away from Hell's Highway and information was soon coming in from Dutch civilians that the Germans were concentrating for an attack at Schijndel. This was 59th Division that was arriving from western Holland via s'Hertogenbosch. At 17.00 hours, the significance of Schijndel was confirmed by a report of the arrival in the town of trucks carrying 2,000 German troops. This was *Kampfgruppe* Huber, a part of 59th Division, supported by four extremely potent *Jagdpanthers* of 1st Company, 559 Panzerjäger Battalion, arriving to join the battle. The force built around two battalions of *Wehrmacht* infantry, was well supported by artillery. Colonel Johnson, however, saw their arrival as another opportunity to destroy a significant enemy force. By advancing, with 1/501 PIR from positions on the Canal near Heeswijk and with 3/501 PIR from Eerde, he planned to drive the enemy into the guns of 502 PIR north of St Oedenrode. Squadrons of British tanks from 44/Royal Tank Regiment (RTR), detached from 4 Armoured Brigade, were to support the two American Regiments; B Squadron with 501 PIR and A Squadron with 502 PIR. C Squadron 15/19 Hussars was divisional reserve. If successful, Colonel Johnson would repeat his previous day's success by enveloping the enemy on a grander scale.

Night 21 - 22 September 1944

The advance began at 19.00 hours, just as Lieutenant Colonel Kinnard was about to conduct a route recce, when he was unexpectedly ordered to 'Move now'. Despite the prospect of a 'night assault on a strange city, filled with an unknown number of enemy', 1/501 PIR set off in column of companies along the road. This was by far the quickest way of covering ground, as a more circumspect advance across country would have bogged down as infantry tried to cross drainage ditches in the darkness. However, in the gathering gloom they were engaged by a vehicle mounted multiple 20mm anti-aircraft gun, supported by a machine gun in a nearby group of houses. The paratroopers took to the drainage ditches and manoeuvred into positions from where, after a sharp firefight, they forced the Germans to

Heavy tank destroyer the *Jagdpanther* – an 88mm gun mounted on a MkV chassis.

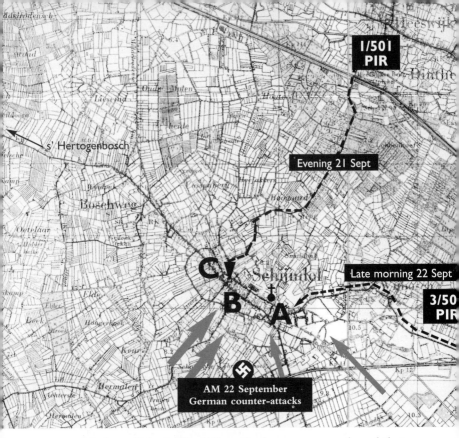

withdraw. Private First Class Beckerman remembered that:

> *'We were crossing many open fields under German fire, hearing the small arms fire whizzing by and making a thud sound as they hit the ground near you. Luckily, none of them had my name on them. I remember chasing a group down the road. They had a 20mm anti-aircraft gun. They would stop around a bend and wait for us to come near, fire a clip point blank at us and then take off.'*

The 1st Battalion's two mile advance, with fixed bayonets, was completed without significant incident by midnight The battalion found the town held by only a few surprised Germans and was secured by 01.50 hours. Colonel Johnson said,

> *'The large German groups, reported earlier, had evidently moved on to the south'.*

At his request, members of the resistance set out on their bicycles on highly dangerous missions to locate the enemy. Meanwhile, the Dutch Resistance reported that the 3rd

Battalion, advancing on Schijndel from Eerde, would encounter a 'sizable blocking force at the railway station'. This position took some time to overcome and the withdrawing Germans mounted a determined resistance. 3/501 PIR finally arrived in Schijndel well after dawn. Sergeant Chapman wrote about dawn on 22 September: 'We took the town filled with enemy soldiers. In the morning, [heavy sleeping!] Krauts came out of bedrooms to walk into our guys in the kitchen.' The town' perimeter bristled with paratroopers and Private Carpenter recalled how:

'In the morning, we set up some roadblocks on the roads leading into Schijndel from the north, east and west. These started paying dividends right away as word hadn't gotten back to the German vehicles as they arrived in that little town.'

Lieutenant Howard and his platoon from Company C 'was having a field day against enemy vehicles coming in from the west'. He urged his men to 'Shoot high so you can knock off those men without ruining a good motor car'. Transport, almost any transport, was useful to paratroopers who could otherwise only manoeuvre at walking pace.

Much of the action described in the next section took place on the southern outskirts of Schijndel. Sadly, post-war development has covered the exact scene but by driving to the edge of the town the ground across which the Germans approached the town can be seen.

Schijndel – Friday 22 September 1944

While Company C was busy capturing unsuspecting Germans arriving in from s'Hertogenbosch, the enemy facing the rest of 1/501PIR, were only too aware of American occupation of the town. This was not a good omen for Colonel Johnson's plan to envelop them.

At 07.15 hours, Company B on the southern edge of the town reported the arrival of a force of 'two hundred infantry supported by two tanks' – these were probably two of the *Jagdpanthers* seen the previous evening. Outnumbered, Company B was soon in trouble, with its forward platoon being driven in. Lieutenant Colonel Kinnard called for fire support but the observer in the church spire, could see nothing through the early autumn ground mist. The *Jagdpanthers*, being even heavier than the Allied Shermans, at forty-seven tons, were confined to the road and advanced to within two-hundred yards of the paratroopers' roadblocks at the town's edge. With the words, 'We're heading that way. I think we can get them from the flank', Company B commander, Lieutenant Hamilton, led his reserve platoon forward. His idea, recorded in the after-action report:

> 'was to make an end run around the buildings to his right, emerge on the line of the enemy advance between the main body and the advance party, take the latter in the rear and so bring the whole movement into check.'

Moving through a nunnery and farm buildings, Lieutenant Hamilton positioned a section to pin down the enemy's main body while his other two sections dealt with the leading group of Germans. Shooting the lock off a large gate, the Screaming Eagles emerged into the street, taking the cautiously advancing enemy force by surprise. Ten Germans were shot down and with the Americans unexpectedly in their rear; the remaining twenty promptly surrendered. The advance of the enemy main body had been halted by manoeuvre tactics. Lieutenant Hamilton's action had stopped a significantly superior force without resorting to an inevitably costly positional defence.

Elsewhere in Schijndel, 1/501 PIR's positions were penetrated and the situation was only restored, at 09.30 hours

German *Fallschirmjäger* on foot move forward to cut off Hell's Highway.

by the arrival of 3/501 PIR. Meanwhile Company A in the eastern part of the town came under attack from an enemy force advancing up the Koveringse Dike road. The tanks were kept at bay by bazooka fire; however, groups of infantry, using the cover of ditches and buildings, infiltrated into the town but never assembled in sufficient strength to hold their gains against the Americans.

With the Germans driven out of their footholds in the town and the Americans lacking sufficient combat power to drive them off, a stalemate developed. The German armour shelled the Americans, who replied with bazooka rounds. The arrival of Colonel Johnson and a squadron of tanks from B Squadron 44/RTR promptly improved the situation. Also, the morning mist had burnt off and the 101st's artillery came into action from the area of St Oedenrode, while themselves being in danger of attack.

According to 44/RTR's Intelligence Officer, Captain Joe Arsenault:

> 'B Squadron had started their southerly move from Schijndel by brassing up some ammo trucks – much to the annoyance of the paratroopers, who wanted to use them as transport – but later were engaged by some 88mm guns from the left flank. These were smartly dealt with by the para-boys who bazooka'd the guns and shot the crews.'

Clearing the Germans away from Schijndel had badly delayed 501 PIR's advance from their line of departure on the railway line to the south of the town but, as recorded by the divisional historian,

> 'The 1st Battalion drew abreast of 3rd along the railroad line at 1330 and the attack jumped off. The 3rd Battalion was well to the left of the highway, but as the ground was perfectly flat, the gap between the two battalions did not become a source of trouble. Advance was swift. From behind the infantry, the [British] tanks engaged the German strong points. As fast as these were softened up the [American] infantry groups moved up their ditches to places where they could be brought under small-arms fire, or wracked with grenades, and then overwhelm them. In the first hour twenty-five enemy were killed … and forty-five captured, with a loss to that [1st] battalion of only eight casualties though the men had been on the go for twenty-four hours, this was heady stuff.'

Soldiers of the 101st escorting a group of German prisoners

At 14.30 hours, with 501 and 502 PIR and their British armour, poised to spring their trap and encircle the enemy between Schijndel and St Oedenrode, news came that the enemy had cut Hell's Highway north east of Veghel. As the 101st's divisional historian said: *'Thus D Plus 5* [22 September], *rather than being the story of a successful attack, became the story of a desperate defence ... to ward off disaster'*. The Allied advance was halted and 501 PIR withdrew back to Schijndel, taking with them one hundred and twenty-five prisoners; a mixed bag from the German 1 *Fallschirmjäger* Regiment and the 49th and 59th Grenadier Divisions. Schijndel had to be abandoned, necessitating its recapture by British units in the coming days. However, keeping Hell's Highway open was 101st Airborne's mission, not

154

Potential for disaster, XXX Corps trucks, bonnet to tailgate, on the single road which would become known as 'Hell's Highway'.

necessarily holding ground on the flanks. It was therefore, vital that Veghel was held and Colonel Johnson ordered 3/501 PIR to move to Eerde immediately and,

> *'In an unusual military movement Colonel Ewell halted his battalion's attack, had all his men execute left face, and walked them off the battlefield with their right flank entirely exposed. The Germans by that time were so disorganized that the battalion got away with it.'*

This withdrawal left 1/501 PIR very exposed and they had a difficult time getting back to Schijndel but by 18.00 hours, they were abandoning the town, leaving behind 170 wounded Germans that had been captured during the day.

CHAPTER TEN

VEGHEL – CLOSURE OF HELL'S HIGHWAY
Hell's Highway is cut at a vital moment

From Schijndel, return to **Veghel**, initially retracing the route out of town. Turn **right** at the roundabout with the steel sculpture following signs to **Veghel**. Re-crossing the Canal Bridge turn **right** at the **first traffic lights** signposted towards **Erp** and Boekel on **Erpsweg**. Park outside the town.

Friday 22 September 1944

The third and, probably, most significant cut of Hell's Highway in the battle so far, took place on D Plus 5. Already, 107 Panzer Brigade's two attacks on 19 and 20 September had significantly, and perhaps fatally, delayed the development of MARKET GARDEN by preventing the timely reinforcement and re-supply of Guards Armoured Division's attack on Nijmegen's Waal Bridges. With crossings of the Waal secure, this closure of Hell's Highway on 22 September starved 43rd Wessex Division of supplies, and had a significant effect on the attack across the Island to Arnhem. Traffic was halted on Hell's Highway and the supply columns and reinforcements necessary to sustain them in offensive operations were at a halt.

In accordance with *Generaloberst* Student's wishes, 59th Division's *Kampfgruppe* Huber, supported by troops from other formations, including *Fallschirmjäger* were preparing to attack Hell's Highway from the west. However, the operations, described in the previous chapter, between Veghel, Schijndel and St Oedenrode by 501 and 502 PIR disrupted this part of the German plan. In addition, *Oberstleutnant* von der Hydte's 6 *Fallschirmjäger* Regiment was delayed and only joined the later stages of the battle. However, the attack mounted from the east by the divisional strength *Kampfgruppe* Walther, under control of LXXVI Corps, was far more successful. This was largely because the over extended 101st, as the after-action report highlights found it 'impossible to be strong everywhere'. In fact, on the morning of 22 September, the only US paratroopers north of Veghel were the, company strength, leading elements of 506 PIR.

157

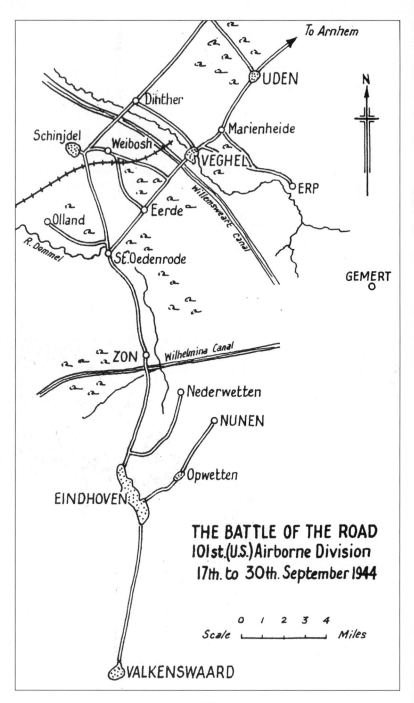

To Arnhem

UDEN

Dinther

Schinjdel

Weibosh

Marienheide

VEGHEL

ERP

Olland

Eerde

R. Dommel

St. Oedenrode

GEMERT

Willemsweart Canal

ZON   Wilhelmina Canal

Nederwetten

NUNEN

Opwetten

EINDHOVEN

THE BATTLE OF THE ROAD
101st.(U.S.) Airborne Division
17th. to 30th. September 1944

0 1 2 3 4
Scale └──┴──┴──┴──┘ Miles

VALKENSWAARD

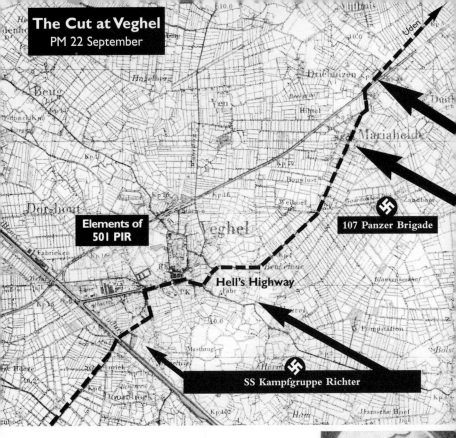

The Cut at Veghel
PM 22 September

Elements of 501 PIR

Veghel

Hell's Highway

107 Panzer Brigade

SS Kampfgruppe Richter

As dawn on 22 September approached, *Kampfgruppe* Walther had assembled its mixed grouping of troops. Forming up astride the Gemert to Erp road were SS-*Hauptsturmführer* Richter's battalion of SS infantry, (1/22 SS Panzer Grenadiers) detached from 10th *Frundsberg* SS Panzer Division. Two companies were to lead the attack, supported by six *Wehrmacht* Panthers, detached from 107 Panzer Brigade. Richter's third and weakest company was to attack Veghel along the road on the northern bank of the canal, along with three of Roestel's SS Stug IV assault guns from their own division. An armoured engineer company mounted in half-tracks, also detached from 107 Panzer Brigade, were following in reserve, acting

SS-*Hauptsturmführer* Richter, commander of 1/22 SS Panzer Grenadiers.

as infantry. SS-*Obersturmführer* Heinz Damaske, Richter's adjutant, described the ground across which the SS-*Kampfgruppe* would attack:

> *'The terrain was unfavourable, 700 to 800 metres of practically no cover over meadowland, then thick scrub with the occasional tree for something like a half-kilometre to the Uden Veghel road.'*

In addition, the Aa's flood plain provided limited armoured manoeuvre corridors.

On higher ground to the north, *Kampfgruppe* Walther's main armoured strength was to approach Veghel from the north-east. This group was based on the Panther and panzer grenadier battalions of Major von Maltzahn's 107 Panzer Brigade, who despite the two actions at the Son Bridge were still at ninety percent of its original strength.

Oberst Walther's aim was to capture Veghel, blow the four bridges and block the road, long enough, for the Allied divisions to the north to be destroyed. Even if they could not hold Veghel itself for long, the Germans believed the destruction of the bridges would impose vital delay to reinforcements. With only logistic traffic on the Corridor, SS-*Obersturmführer* Damaske recorded that,

> *'the enemy had obviously not noticed the forming up point and on both sides of the* [Gemert to Erp] *road, we quickly made progress against weak resistance'.*

Erp was captured, the advance continued, and *Kampfgruppe* Walther soon established itself on two miles, of Hell's Highway, immediately north of Veghel. At 11.00 hours, with plumes of smoke from burning trucks marking the area of attack, 107 Panzer Brigade and SS-*Hauptsturmführer* Richter's *Kampfgruppe* prepared to launch the final phase of their attack by assaulting Veghel and its bridges. And then the Allied reinforcements arrived.

Return to Veghel and turn right (north) on the **N265** towards **Uden**. 107 Panzer Brigade occupied the road in the area of **Mariaheide** and advanced on Veghel astride the road. Pass through **Mariaheide** and turn off the main road onto **Hoogsraat**. Park here. This is the site of the level crossing that the Guards reached on the evening of 22 September 1944.

British and American troops bailed out of Jeeps and trucks as Germans shell.

The British Reaction

Kampfgruppe Walther had struck a nose to tail stream of XXX Corps vehicles on Hell's Highway. Lieutenant Colonel McCance, the officer responsible for supplying 43rd Wessex Division recorded how:

> *'... the Divisional B Echelon, reinforced by Corps [logistic] troops, was split by the German road block between Veghel and Uden on 22nd September. We lost a significant number of our undefended RASC vehicles – there were no troops piqueting the route and precious few escorts. Club Route was closed for twenty-five hours and, consequently, the supply situation on the Island became critical. I am convinced that this prevented an early crossing of the Rhine by the Division to relieve the Airborne.'*

Confusion reigned. The streets of Veghel were choked, with cumbersome and heavily laden vehicles; many with convoy commanders killed or stranded the other side of the German roadblock.

While news of the cut had reached 501 PIR by 14.30 hours, it was later in the afternoon that word of the cut in the vital Corridor reached Lieutenant General Horrocks at Malden, on the outskirts of Nijmegen. For General Horrocks:

> '...the 22nd was a bad day for me. I had witnessed the failure of 214 Brigade [43rd Division on The Island], and no advance had been made anywhere on XXX Corps front. I arrived at my headquarters to be told by my BGS [Brigadier General Staff] that contact had now been made at last with 1st Airborne ... their situation could hardly have been worse. While I was pondering over this information, my BGS returned to say that once more, a German armoured formation had succeeded in cutting our road to the rear. There was only one thing for it – I ordered the 32nd Guards Brigade to turn back and open the road by attacking from the north.'

A 4/Wilts (43 Wessex Division) carrier waiting for the road ahead to be cleared.

Uden →

Site of railway line

As far as the Grenadiers reached on the evening of 22 September. The site of rail crossing on the road to Uden.

That evening XXX Corps's AQ War Diary recorded.

> *'Enemy succeeded in cutting Corps L of C in area VEGHEL 4838, resulting in complete hold up of all movement'.*

By 17.30 hours, 32 Guards Brigade, with the Grenadier and Coldstream Guards Groups under command, were moving back south down Hell's Highway, at a time when it was vital that attention and resources needed to be concentrated on reaching Arnhem. A Squadron 2/HCR was also recalled from a task on the flanks and arrived to support 32 Guards Brigade. The Grenadiers Group, led by a troop of No. 1 Squadron's Shermans, accompanied by a platoon of infantry from No. 4 Company moved south. The divisional historian recorded that,

> *'The Group's journey to Uden was eventful only by reason of the little clusters of Dutch people who congregated in the villages to watch the tanks go by, obviously believing that the liberation had come to an untimely end'.*

The historian continues:

> *'Uden was a strange sight. American paratroopers had set up headquarters in the school, and a small Stars and Stripes fluttered from the window. RASC lorries, which had been hurrying back to collect more supplies, were parked in every street. Staff officers sat mournfully in their cars, waiting to take reports from the front line to their generals. If they had been passengers on a Tube* [underground or metro railway] *stuck between two stations, this odd assortment of stragglers from the British and American Armies could not have looked more annoyed.'*

Passing through Uden, confirmation of the northern enemy

Re opening
Hell's Highway
23 September 1944

SS Kampfgruppe
and Fallschirmjäger
AM 23 September

327
GIR

F Coy.

B Sqn 44/RTR

2/506 PIR

1/506
PIR

2/501
PIR

C Sqn 44/RTR
327 GIR

3/502
PIR

Fallschirmjäger
AM 23 September

positions was made when the Grenadiers lost a scout car to a
Panzerfaust at the level crossing two miles to the south.
However, in the gathering darkness little could be achieved
beyond recce and preparing a hasty defence to prevent the
enemy moving north.

Meanwhile Captain the Honourable Willouhby's company of
Coldstream Guards along with a troop of tanks operating to the
east of Hell's Highway located a vast German ration store at
Oss, containing over a million man days of rations. While XXX

Corps may have been starved of ammunition, fuel and engineer stores, they certainly did not go hungry, although many complained about the black bread and *Wurst*. Many units record incidents at Oss and all mention the phlegmatic Dutch store keeper. According to XXX Corps historian:

'He was a pleasant old man, only too willing to issue the supplies to anyone who was willing to sign for them. ... the quartermasters were drawing their needs and signing with pleasure. But it came as a shock to one QM, who, as he was signing, noticed that the signature previous to his own was that of a German Captain. The ancient custodian cheerfully agreed that this was correct, and thereafter his staff was increased by a party of Tommies.'

Others recall tacit agreements where the British drew rations from one end of the massive depot while the Germans drew theirs from the opposite end!

The American Reaction

Overnight 21/22 September, 101st Airborne Division's intelligence officers had been nervously assessing the significance of reports from the Dutch Underground of German forces massing to the east and west of the Corridor. As it seemed likely that the enemy attack would strike the undefended portion of Hell's Highway north of Veghel, plans were made for 506 PIR to move up the route to Uden as soon as they were relieved in Eindhoven. The imminent attack brought forward the time of the move. Under Lieutenant Colonel Chase, a mixture of units based on Regimental Headquarters moved off just before 10.00 hours:

> 'Riding trucks and every other kind of vehicle that could be got, the advance party... managed to get to Uden by 11.00. Right after it passed, the Germans cut the road north of Veghel, and it was isolated [from the remainder of the Division] until 1700 the next day.'

107 Panzer Brigade, prevented all but a few members of 506 PIR from reaching Uden. Colonel Chase and a hundred and fifty men took up positions in the deserted town. He recalled,

> 'Had the Germans realized that my force consisted only of Regimental Headquarters Company and a platoon from the 2nd Battalion, the Germans might have overwhelmed us.'

The divisional historian recorded how in the ensuing fight as the panzer grenadiers probed his defences:

> 'It was touch and go all the time, but Colonel Chase made masterful use of his meagre forces, rushing them back and forth across town, firing, creating an impression of strength. And the Germans never went all out against them.'

However, to be fair to the Germans, the force facing Uden was only a flank protection detachment designed to prevent the Allies from the north interfering with 107 Panzer Brigade's main effort against Veghel.

To the south, while 1st and 3/501 PIR were still attempting their envelopment movements around Schijndel (see Chapter 9), 2/501 PIR was holding Veghel. Private First Class Cartledge

A Browning Automatic Rifle (BAR) .30 calibre, was standard issue to all US Army infantry squads.

recalled how his patrol on Hell's Highway:

'... was walking down the road from our outpost to four [British] trucks with 40mm anti-aircraft guns behind and the men had stopped for tea. I explained that we five men were the only Americans within a half-mile or so, and the enemy could see them from the distance. The British [Artillery] captain told this American private how presumptuous I was to tell him what to do. Frank "Chief" Sayers laughed ... and said, "Well you told him." ... In about ten minutes, all hell broke loose and we helped evacuate the bodies and the wounded much later. The trucks and guns burned all that afternoon.'

On the eastern outskirts of Veghel, reports of the approach of forty Panthers brought reinforcements hurrying to meet the enemy. For a time, the paratroopers were on their own facing the enemy. Private Derber recalled:

'We pulled out of our positions and forced marched across town to meet them. ... a German machine gun opened up on us and I saw the tracers coming at us and hitting the dirt not 15 feet away. I hit the dirt too and tried to locate the enemy so I could take him out with my .03 rifle with a grenade launcher and five rifle grenades. ... A few riflemen came to join us and formed a Line of Resistance and a German tank appeared in the far corner of the field. My assistant gunner manned the LMG [light machine gun] while I prepared to use my grenade launcher on the tank. A burst from a BAR to my right caused the tank commander to button up and a nearby rifleman was lobbing rifle grenades at the tank so I saved mine.'

SS-Obersturmführer Damske was on the receiving end of the fire:

'Further progress through this marshy terrain was not possible. Moreover, the engineers and panzer-grenadiers came

With few vehicles, the main body of 506 PIR move north on foot towards Uden.

under well-aimed rifle fire delivered by the American paratroopers and were not able to take a further step forward.'

With their accompanying riflemen pinned down by the paratroopers, the panzers did not press home their attack. Meanwhile heavier Allied reinforcements started to arrive. Brigadier General Higgins recorded:

'Battery B, 81/Anti-Tank Battalion arrived and went into action on the highway and immediately destroyed a Mark V tank leading the attack. The 2nd Battalion 506th took position on the left of the 2nd Battalion 501st , with 3rd Battalion 327th Glider Infantry on its left. With assistance of the British artillery gathered from the highway, the attack from Erp was repulsed by dark.'

This omits the fact that C Squadron 44/RTR was speedily redeployed from Schindel and, along with rocket-firing RAF Typhoons, played a significant part in helping the lightly armed paratroopers halt the attack within sight of the Veghel bridges. SS-*Obersturmführer* Damske recalled the intervention of the Allied fire support, particularly the artillery:

'... the English then fired a protective barrage out of all available barrels, including smoke, particularly in Richter's sector. At the same time the attack [by 107 Panzer Brigade] along the main road stalled against formidable tank units.'

With the Allied strength building, SS-*Hauptsturmführer* Richter, according to SS-*Obersturmführer* Damaske;

'changed his attack plan, which he now felt to be totally impractical He decided that fire now had to be opened from the flank against the [Allied] armoured forces moving on the Veghel

168

road. The canal bridge came under fire from the Sturmgeschütz [tracked assault guns] *from the line we had reached.'*

Richter had succeeded in cutting Hell's Highway by fire but 107 Panzer Brigade were astride the road, attempting to take Veghel by attacking south down the road through Mariaheide. However, they were halted by Allied firepower and failed in their primary aim of capturing and blowing the Veghel bridges. Brigadier General McAuliffe who had arrived in Veghel to find a new location for divisional HQ, was tasked by General Taylor to take responsibility of co-ordinating the town's defence and reopening Hell's Highway. He disposed his troops in a defence in depth but by last light, Veghel was still the scene of bitter fighting. Sergeant Taylor of Company F, 2/506 PIR wrote:

Hold up down the line. 1st Airborne Division's Sea-Tail halted on Hell's Highway. Crews rest up whilst the Screaming Eagles and the Guards fight to clear the way.

Soldiers of the 101st Airborne take cover as convoys from XXX Corps come under enemy fire.

'During the night we could hear tanks moving around in front of us and we told our people not to open fire unless they had to. We decided to move a machine gun out there in the middle of the night, as I crawled up through some bushes, I put my hand on someone's leg and sort of froze momentarily. I knew he was alive, whoever it was, and in a second I heard someone say in a British voice, "Are you American or German?" There were two British soldiers who had been hiding in the ditch since that episode that afternoon and they were pretty shook up and scared.'

Elsewhere in the town, General McAulliffe ordered XXX Corps' 3.7 and 4.5-inch anti-aircraft crews back to their guns in an unfamiliar anti-tank role. Much to the Gunners' surprise, their guns, which had almost exactly the same characteristics as the German 88mm, were extremely successful and as a result, this Regiment ended the war with more tank than aircraft kills! On the few occasions, normally in extremis, when the British used their anti-aircraft guns against tanks the results were promising but there was no move to mount these guns in tanks or tank destroyers.

After dark, Private Zimmermman was given a message to send from the Division's forward Command Post over his SRC-499 radio set to XXX Corps:

> 'to get help from the "Desert Rats" [7th British Armoured Division]. The reception was bad. Two people came to check to see if the message got through. I had so much trouble, I told one of them to be quiet. It turned out to be General McAuliffe! If I hadn't gotten through, I guess my tail would have been mud. The general understood and thanked me.'

As the Americans struggled to defend the vital Veghel bridges, small parties of Germans closed in to the town from the south and west, almost surrounding the town. Amongst these were 59th Division's *Kampfgruppe* Huber and the footsore *Fallschirmjäger* of *Oberstleutnant* Von der Hydte's 6 *Fallschirmjäger* Regiment, whose attack from the west, at one point, came dangerously close to the railway bridges. Huber's force was virtually surrounded and destroyed, as American paratroopers from across the division moved towards Veghel.

SS-*Obersturmführer* Damaske summed up the situation after *Kampfgruppe* Richter's final assault on Veghel:

> 'This attack also broke apart under the heaviest artillery fire we had experienced since Eterville and Hill 112 in northern France, a superiority of material we could not match. Even during darkness and long after the attack had come to a halt, our positions were hammered without pause by artillery, which had no regard for ammunition expenditure rates. While this was going on, the infantry in the first company who had been set in defence were reduced to getting a few belts of machine gun ammunition passed on from the panzer crews, in order to carry on fighting.'

While the SS infantry and the well protected Panthers stood their ground, some of *Oberst* Walther's *Wehrmacht* troops were withdrawing. Damaske continues,

> 'The situation is confused. The armoured Engineer Company has broken off the action and some of its half-tracks are driving eastwards; they could not be pressured into remaining any longer'.

The situation was not looking hopeful for the Germans but every hour they blocked Hell's Highway, vital supplies were denied to the Allied divisions fighting to the north.

Fallschirmjäger examine a British armoured car on Hell's Highway.

Oberstleutnant von der Heydte, Commander of the 6 *Fallschirmjäger* Regiment.

Fallschirmjäger Renew the Attack

The advance of VIII British Corps to the east of Hell's Highway threatened the left flank of *Kampfgruppe* Walther However, the Germans renewed their attack at dawn on 23 September but this time from the west. *Oberstleutnant* von der Heydte's inexperienced and mainly young soldiers of 6 *Fallschirmjäger* Regiment were now fully concentrated and prepared to renew the battle. However, in his opinion,

'the training and combat experience of the troops were inadequate to meet the requirements of such an attack'.

Still missing promised SS Infantry and assault guns, von der Heydte admitted that he,

'went about the execution of the task given to my regiment with little hope of success'.

None the less, his action delayed the American counter-attack to reopen the highway, for additional precious hours.

Supported by heavy mortar fire, 6 *Fallschirmjäger* Regiment's attack fell on 2/501 to the south of Veghel. With only the hastiest reconnaissance and the briefest of orders the footsore *Fallschirmjäger* advanced through an area of scrub and one of the two battalions emerged onto an open area where there was 'hardly any cover'. *Oberstleutnant* von der Hydte, forward with one of his battalions, realized that

'*the attack was hopelessly stalled, and that it would be impossible to seize and retain Eerde, much less the Veghel Bridge, with the force already committed*'.

Having called back a battalion that had become disorientated in the scrubby terrain, the *Fallschirmjäger* were digging-in by 12.00 hours.

By 13.00 hours, the missing 9th SS (*Hohenstaufen*) Panzer Division's battalion of infantry under SS-*Hauptsturmführer* Segler and *Obersturmführer* Roestel's dozen assault guns had arrived and renewed the attack. However, 1/501 PIR's defences were well organized and supported by both XXX Corps and 101st Divisions' artillery. Consequently, the SS attack soon ground to a halt.

The American Counter-Attack from the South – 23 September 1944

With the failure of the SS and 6 *Fallschirmjäger* Regiment's attacks from the south-west, the situation, as far as the Allies were concerned, was stabilized and operations to restore the vital link to the north could get under away. The Divisional counter-attack plan was for 506 PIR, with the Shermans of B

A German photograph of British scout cars burning on Hell's Highway after being knocked out by German anti-tank fire.

Germans with knocked out vehicles on Hell's Highway. September 22 and 23, 1944

Squadron 44/RTR, to attack northwards on Hell's Highway to meet a southerly thrust by 32 Guards Brigade. Meanwhile, C Squadron 44/RTR along with elements of 327 GIR were to advance east to clear the enemy from Erp. A Squadron 44/RTR joined elements of 501 PIR holding the Eerde sector to the south west of Veghel, to prevent renewed attacks by *Oberstleutnant* von der Hydte.

As 506 PIR was moving to its line of departure, the last combat elements of the 101st finally arrived in seventy-seven gliders of the much-delayed fourth lift at LZ W, between Son and St Oedenrode. Their arrival further enhanced the Allied firepower, with the 105mm guns of 907/Glider Field Artillery Battalion and support elements of 327 GIR being available to join the battle. In addition, during the day, the 101st's Sea Tail of non-airportable and non-essential vehicles arrived to complete the Division's order of battle. Reports to the German LXXXVIII Korps of the arrival of further American reinforcements prompted the following order:

> '*Divisions are to implement draconian measures and be merciless in their quest to provide reserves again, even so called stragglers are to be reformed in this role under tight control.*'

It would seem that even the German genius in mounting an effective defence with *ad hoc* units and formations was wearing thin. German commanders complained that there was a serious gulf between the stream of instructions emanating from superior headquarters and the reality on the ground.

At 14.00 hours, 2/506 PIR started their advance north up Hell's Highway to Uden. Company F, 2/506 PIR were first to suffer casualties. Sergeant Schwenk recalled that:

> *'Our platoon leader was visibly shaken. What we got from him was that our platoon was to lead the attack – right smack into the Germans and their tanks. This was his death warrant. The road on which we were to move was strewn with wreckage from a British convoy, which the Jerries had smashed the day before. The trucks were still burning.'*

Company F's advance had only just begun, when a quietly burning British truck exploded, killing the platoon leader who had been so shaken by his orders.

The paratrooper's advance halted in disorder and the tanks of 107 Panzer Brigade counter-attacked. Sergeant Schwenk recalled what happened:

> *'I couldn't believe my eyes. Three Panther tanks came rolling down the road towards us – all guns blazing. 75mm shells exploding on the road. Smaller turret guns swinging and firing continuously. This was not a good place to be. We had some cover, as the roadside ditches were about two feet deep. ... The tank was almost between us. I could count the bolts on the tread. There was a .57mm anti-tank gun back aways. ... just then the gun fired and nailed the tank spinning him to the left. The*

The supplementary bridge over the canal at Veghel.

disabled tank turned into a field and began to burn. The men who tried to crawl out of the turret were easy targets for our guys. I noticed the other two tanks had turned back – they had no infantry with them.'

The arrival of the Shermans of B Squadron 44/RTR stabilized the situation but, as Sergeant Taylor recalled:

'It was now about 3 o'clock that afternoon and we eventually got word to move out. We went straight up the highway. We didn't meet anything. We went up a few miles and took a road to the right and I was moving along a ditch through an orchard area. We spotted a German half-track out there several hundred yards. We were going around in the hope of cutting that dude off and ... all of a sudden an enemy officer raised up in front of me. ... He was hollering "Kamerad, Kamerad, Kamerad".'

Shortly afterwards, British Shermans were seen approaching from the north.

32 Guards Brigade's attack 23 September

Attacking from the north the Guard's plan was simple. The Grenadiers were to force their way south through the two thousand yards of German held road to meet up with the Americans. Meanwhile, the Coldstream Guards were to advance on the road that runs east from Uden to deal with enemy concentrated in Volkel. With radio communication working well, fire support was to come from south of the cut.

The start of the Guard's attack was delayed so that it could be co-ordinated with that of 506 PIR from Veghel. However, when it eventually got going, the Grenadiers found that the majority of the enemy had melted away. The heavy fire from the artillery overnight and the renewed fighting on the morning of 23 September had sapped the strength of 107 Panzer Brigade, which was in the unenviable position of facing two fronts. Major von Maltzahn's command again proved that it lacked the stomach for a sustained fight. However, the Coldstream Group met stiffer opposition at Volkel.

Lieutenant Franklin had led his troop of A Squadron 2/HCR towards Volkel. Corporal-of-Horse Booth recalled:

'Lieutenant Franklin had halted the troop and we were all in a position to observe a line of 88-mm guns in a row. These guns were partially concealed by an embankment a kilometre to our east at a place called Oosterens. ... Lieutenant Franklin duly

Mk V Panther tank with its high velocity 75mm gun. Note the track links attached as additional armour.

reported his findings and the troop was ordered to keep the enemy guns in sight and await the arrival of the Coldstreamers, who were coming forward with tanks and infantry.'

While the cavalrymen were observing the enemy, a C-47 with glider heading north to 82nd Airborne's LZ north of the Waal crash-landed in their position. Corporal-of-Horse Booth continued his account:

'Within a short time, fourteen paratroopers in the most spotless order... came over towards us. This was their third attempt to get to Nijmegen, they said, as they had to turn back owing to weather being so bad. ... I have never seen anything like their kit. They had jeeps, rifles, grenades hung all over them, chewing gum, and even brand new frying pans. "Say, boys, which way to the battle?" demanded one. We pointed in the direction of the 88mms and warned them that there were a number about. We also suggested that they should be careful about showing themselves and that we had been ordered to await the arrival of reinforcements. "Say, Buddy, we came here to fight and that's what we're going to do." With which remark the entire party motored off towards the enemy. ... we saw them

LITTER
OF
CRASHED
GLIDERS

MEDIUM
ARTILLERY
FIRING.

BRITISH
GRAVES.

ARMOURED
BULLDOZER.

BULLDOZER ON
CONVEYOR.

DUCK'S

PRESS

DISPATCH
RIDER.

disappear round a bend in the road. All at once, there was a
tremendous burst of firing and the sound of loud explosions and
much shouting. After an interval the survivors came back ...'
The cavalrymen had even less success in persuading the
Coldstream Guards to be cautious:

178

'Lieutenant Franklin supplied the commander of the first tank with all the information he had, and also told him what had happened to the Americans but he formed the impression that his story was not entirely credited. There was a brief conference and the first tanks went into the attack. Straightaway three went up

Gun crew of a German 88 preparing a new position for iminent action: stabilizing legs are being secured, ammunition pits and slit trenches dug.

in quick succession and the attack stopped dead.'

The Coldstream Group's Fifth Battalion was short of infantry and was organized in two companies but the First Battalion's tank strength was still ninety percent. In these circumstances, Number 3 Squadron's tanks, unsupported by infantry, had led the way in the first abortive attack on Volkel. As 107 Panzer Brigade had earlier found, infantry support was necessary in such difficult terrain. As indicated by Corporal-of-Horse Booth,

the renewed attack was better planned and supported:

'There was another O Group at the side of the road, then the column got under way once more, supported by 3" mortars and infantry.'

At ten minutes past one, attacking together, Number 1 Squadron and Number 1 Company overcame the German anti-tank screen with machine gun and mortar fire. At long ranges, the 88mm was supreme against the lightly armoured Allied tanks. However, deployed in the open, the high silhouette of the dual purpose anti aircraft/tank gun and lack of protection for the gun crews was a significant weakness in close-quarter fighting with enemy infantry. With the way open to Volkel the Company/Squadron group closed in on the village.

The light armour of 2/HCR was left covering the flanks and watched the Coldstreamers attack:

'The Germans replied with mortars and the Coldstream casualties began to trickle back in growing numbers. Then in a further five minutes or so there was even more noise – lots of bangs, shouts and explosions as the Foot Guards got in amongst the Germans with their bayonets, then silence, and shortly afterwards people began to filter back along the road. An officer remarked that "Seven Panther tanks had just got away and were hovering about".'

The Company Squadron Group having driven off the Panthers had to keep them at bay, while the infantry, supported by a proportion of the Squadron's Shermans, had to clear the panzer grenadiers from Volkel. Leaving his squadron second-in-

Britsh column led by a Bren-gun carrier moving up the road towards Nijmegen.

command to fight the armoured battle outside the village, Major Darell joined the infantry company commander, Major The Lord Long, who had only taken over Number 1 Company the day before. Working together on foot, the two commanders would be better able to co-ordinate the clearance of the village. In understatement typical of the Guards, the Coldstream's historian described the battle as 'a bitter little fight' but what it lacked in scale, it certainly made up for in intensity.

The sturdy brick-built Dutch houses made excellent

positions for the Germans who had to be driven out of successive buildings. The Guards infantry and armour, which were well used to working together, cleared through the village in a thoroughly competent manner. However, Lord Long was killed while directing his platoons from a forward position and following further officer casualties, Company Sergeant Major Farnhill commanded the final stages of the battle. Farnhill won a well deserved Distinguished Conduct Medal, while a Sergeant and a Guardsman each earned a Military Medal. The regimental historian concluded that:

'By 3 o'clock the village was clear. It remained only to beat the woods and villages to the south east, and the tanks sent forward to do this found that the Germans had already withdrawn'

By midnight, XXX Corps' route north was again clear and the enemy had been driven away from positions on the immediate eastern flank from where they would have been able to interfere with the traffic on Hell's Highway. However, with the British VIII Corps advancing more quickly, the Germans were to complete the removal of the eastern threat of their own accord. On the evening of 23 September, LXXXVIII Korps ordered *Kampfgruppe* Walther, who had lost twenty percent of its armour and twenty-five percent of its infantry, to disengage and move to new defensive positions in the Venlo area. The departure of *Kampfgruppe* Walther over the next thirty-six hours, removed the last significant threat to the eastern flank of Hell's Highway.

While the situation had been restored in 101st Airborne Division's area, the situation to the north was still in the balance. Hell's Highway had been closed for thirty-five vital hours on the day the spearhead of 43rd Wessex Division broke out of their bridgehead at Oousterhout on The Island, between the Waal at Nijmegen and the Rhine. In a dash across the Island, 5th Duke of Cornwall's Light Infantry, supported by 4/7 Dragoon Guards, covered ten miles in thirty minutes to reach the Rhine at Driel. With the vital road cut behind them at Veghel and both guns and infantry critically short of ammunition and supplies, the options open to General Horrocks were becoming extremely limited.

501 PIR's memorial at the Windmill at Eerde.

CHAPTER ELEVEN

THE CUT AT KOEVERING
The final cut that crushed Montgomery's dreams

Return to **Veghel** and drive through the town on the **N265** towards Son. A mile after crossing the Canal Bridge take the right turn to **Eerde**. Turn off the main road at the outskirts of Eerde and follow the road through the village and park by the **Memorial and remains of the windmill**. The Eersche Bergen (Eerde Sand Dunes) lie beyond the windmill.

Dawn – 24 September 1944

After a relatively quiet night, the first light of dawn struggled through a gloom of low cloud and rain. On Hell's Highway, XXX Corps traffic crawled forward. Drivers starved of proper rest struggled to keep their eyes open. Royal Army Service Corps driver Stanley Winton of 43 Ordnance Field Park said:

'Since we were ordered on to the Centre Line [on 21 September], *I only had a few hours cat-nap in the cab of my American two and a half ton truck. We were constantly warned to be ready to move but if we moved at all, it would only be for a short distance before we halted again.'*

On the western flank of Hell's Highway, some very tired American paratroopers and Household Cavalrymen of A Squadron 2/HCR were warning that the enemy were massing for an attack. Their positions at Eerde had been probed by

American Airborne troops in Eerde.

German recce patrols, who by nightfall, had a clear picture of the necessarily thin American defences to the west of Hell's Highway. An entry timed 20.25 hours on 23 September, in General Reinhard's LXXXVII Corps's war diary, recorded that:

> 'Recce report Erede is occupied but no enemy reported from Schijndel to Dinther in the north-east.'

Further south there appeared to be gaps in 101st's defences north of St Oedenrode. From Fifteenth Army, orders came down the German chain of command for an attack. Overnight, General Chill moved his headquarters forward to Schijndel and, at dawn, gave his orders for an attack on the Veghel bridges starting at 09.00 hours on 24 September.

General Chill's force had been rushed together from remnants of units that had previously dashed themselves against the American defences and from any 'stragglers' that could be found. The main attack was to be launched by five hundred paratroopers of *Oberstleutnant* von der Heydte's 6 *Fallschirmjäger* Regiment on an axis from Schijndel to the Veghel bridges via Eerde. In reserve were *Kampfgruppe* Jungwirth, which was based on the remnants of *Kampfgruppe* Huber and 1035 Fusilier Regiment.

The Battle for the Eerde Sand Dunes – September

Shortly before 10.00 hours von der Heydte's *Fallschirmjäger* approached Eerde driving in Company C, 1/501 PIR's outposts, which had been positioned in the sand dunes to the northwest of the village. The divisional historian recalled:

> 'The outpost platoon came rushing back with word that the town was about to be attacked by five tanks [assault guns] and two hundred infantry coming down the road from Schijndel. By the time Lieutenant Colonel Kinnard got the report, the enemy was in the dunes, looking down the throats of his men.'

Back at 501 PIR's Regimental Headquarters, Colonel Johnson dispatched his nine remaining Shermans of A Squadron 44/RTR towards Eerde to check the German advance. At the same time, in order to bring effective artillery fire to bear, Lieutenant Howard climbed the Church steeple, despite the attention it was receiving from the enemy tanks. With Allied tanks and artillery now supporting the determined paratroopers, the German advance came to a halt in the sand dunes and, consequently, they attempted to manoeuvre around Eerde. In the battle to

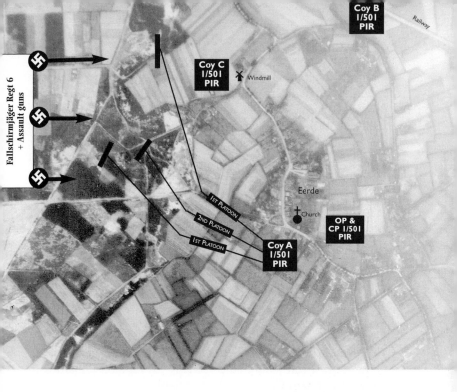

contain the enemy at Eerde, 44/RTR lost a further three precious Shermans. To the north, Company B and neighbouring Company I's (3/501 PIR) overlapping arcs of fire prevented the Germans advancing along the railway line. On the southern flank of the dunes, Company A moved up to clear the sand dunes from their original positions immediately south of the village. 'Captain Stach of A was given a section of light machine guns, a mortar observer and a prayer.' Company C was to form a fire support base from its central position on the crest of the dunes. H Hour was 12.15 and was preceded by a fire-plan shot by the guns of the 101st's artillery reinforced by those of XXX Corps.

Company A was to advance from south-east to north-west. On their left flank, 1st Platoon's second in command, Lieutenant Murphy, led a squad forward to secure a wooded area. At first this advance went well. However, emerging into an open area they came under heavy fire. The squad dived for cover, while Private Belffer ran to a fire position on the left flank. Undaunted by the volume of German fire that was concentrated on him, he shot back, virtually winning the firefight on his own. The rest of

1st Platoon moved up, with the platoon's other machine guns joining Private Belffer to form a fire support group, while the riflemen prepared to attack. The Germans had their heads down, sheltering from the hail of lead and, seizing the moment, Lieutenant Mosier yelled 'Lets go!' The paratroopers ran across the hundred metres of open area, ignoring exploding mortar rounds and machine gun fire. As the highly trained and aggressive American paratroopers closed in, some Germans broke and ran. Working in pairs, the paratroopers flushed the remaining *Fallschirmjäger* out of their shallow trenches, which had been hastily dug in the sandy soil. The ensuing fight had all the frenzy and brutality to be expected when two military élites meet head on. Lieutenant Murphy recalled:

'What we did in those moments we could scarcely remember afterwards because we had no time to think. It was courage such as I have never imagined possible, almost foolish courage, and I doubt if any group of men could have held their ground against us'.

At the end of the battle, there were fifteen dead *Fallschirmjäger* along with seven wounded prisoners. 1st Platoon remained in position to guard Company A's left flank.

2nd Platoon's mission was to advance through the centre of the sand dunes where they also came under small-arms, machine gun and mortar fire, with defenders and attackers exchanging grenades over the scrub covered dunes, as they fought from dune to dune. American covering fire from the

Weary paratroopers of 6 *Fallschirmjäger* Regiment, march forwards to begin the attack.

Platoon's 60mm mortar and machine guns; a wild rush and a bitter close quarter fight, was a recipe repeated until the large central dune was reached. Here the Americans came to a halt, as the Germans had made use of an open area, one hundred yards wide, to produce a wall of fire. The situation for 2nd Platoon, whose leaders had been killed, was made worse when a *Jagdpanther* opened fire on them and the *Fallschirmjäger* counter-attacked. It is entirely to 2nd Platoon's credit that they stood their ground and beat off the enemy. Unable to resume their attack however, they found that they had occupied excellent fire positions, from where they were able to pin down the Germans. They could also act as cut-offs for Lieutenant Mier's 3rd Platoon, who were to come up from reserve and attack on the company's right flank driving the Germans from the large dune into 2nd Platoon's fire.

559/Panzerjäger's Battalion's Attack

Sand dunes are not good tank country and, consequently, the assault guns of 559/*Panzerjäger* Battalion now sought other avenues of approach to the Veghel Bridges. To the north of Eerde, 1 and 3/501 PIR presented a solid front protecting the direct route to their objectives. Therefore, they took the open approach to the south of Eerde and its dunes. In doing so, they destroyed a patrol of three British Shermans sent up from the route north to see what was happening around Eerde. Colonel Kershaw describes the scene as the *panzerjäger* closed in on Hell's Highway.

> 'On the main road, Allied drivers frantically baled out of trucks as the Panzerjäger began machine-gunning and shelling the highway. The ammunition vehicles disintegrated into flaming, spitting pyres as drivers scurried for cover, throwing them selves into roadside ditches. A troop of three British tanks churning down the main road was brewed up, one tank after the other. Within minutes, huge writhing palls of black oily smoke were boiling up into the sky. Traffic to the north jerked to a halt as this awesome spectacle of destruction began to blot out the skies before them. Vulnerable trucks began to jam up nose to tail...'

See Air photo page 195

That a cut had been made was the kind of positive news that General Chill was under pressure to deliver to General Reinhard's LXXXVII Corps. To the north of the Eerde Sand

British ammunition truck on fire after been knocked out by the Jungwirth *Fallschirmjäger* Battalion.

Dunes, Chill was able to report, at 15.00 hours that his troops were, 'within 700 yards of the railway bridge'. However, what he did not report was that a well organized battalion of American paratroopers was standing in his way and that they were showing no signs of being overcome by von der Hydte's 6 *Fallschirmjäger* Regiment. More accurately, he reported that 'So far the Corridor had only been cut by fire south of Eerde'. Two lone assault guns had closed Hell's Highway in the area south of Veghel and by mid-afternoon on 24 September, the vulnerability of the Corridor, only a road's width wide in places, was plain for all to see. Meanwhile, twenty-five miles to the north, XXX Corps was preparing to mount a battalion operation to cross the Rhine with 4/Dorset. In the event of failure, contingency orders had been issued for the evacuation of the British Airborne from the Oosterbeek Perimeter. The cut in XXX Corps' supply route at Koevering was a contributory factor in General Horrocks deciding to seek General Dempsey's confirmation that Operation BERLIN, the evacuation, was to be carried out the following night.

Continue on past the windmill as the main road is approached, turn left onto another minor road (**Dalenstraat**). Turn left onto **Vlangheide** and follow this road through woods that conceal buildings of Cold War vintage. **Turn left** towards **Koevering**. Park before reaching the main **N265**. This is the southern end of the final 'cut'.

Evening 24 September 1944 – The Cut at Koevering

Striking in a south-easterly direction from Schijndel towards Hell's Highway, Major Hans Jungwirth's *Kampfgruppe* avoided contact with the enemy. At 18.00 peering through his field glasses, he saw the column of Allied vehicles halted, nose to tail, on the road north, the route in front of him having been blocked by the fire of the assault guns. Further north Jungwirth's grenadiers, *Fallschirmjäger* and other crews of 559/*Panzerjäger* Battalion prepared to join the action. Orders were hastily given, with arcs of fire and priority targets allocated to individual assault guns. Allied vehicles parked nose to tail, presented an excellent target and resulted in a spectacular conflagration. The flickering light from burning trucks illuminated the night and ammunition 'cooked-off' and shot into the sky. According to the author of XXX Corps' History:

> *'As was only to be expected the enemy's efforts resulted in the capture of a number of vehicles and men. One man, Driver Ferguson, of 536 Company RASC, which was moving up to Nijmegen at the time, managed to elude capture and spent three days and nights in the loft of a house where the enemy set up headquarters. Indeed, one night Driver Ferguson had the company of some German soldiers in the same loft , but managed to hide himself by burrowing into a pile of wheat sacks.'*

News of the arrival of German armour and infantry on Hell's Highway at Koevering was received with consternation amongst the Allies at St Oedenrode. 502 PIR had only a few anti-tank guns but 907th Glider Field Artillery (GFA) Battalion was within four hundred yards of the nearest burning trucks. Lieutenant Colonel Nelson promptly ordered Battery B to be

Trucks destroyed and pushed into a ditch at Koevering.

A German self-propelled gun captured at Koevering. The armament is a short barrelled 75mm gun and it was used in close support of infantry.

deployed in the ground defence role, while Battery A was to continue firing in support of 501 PIR at Eerde. Captain McGlone, Battery B commander, immediately ordered the guns out of their deep pits from which they could only provide conventional indirect fire support. Deploying to cover the approaches to St Oedenrode with direct fire, McGlone bolstered his line with

> *'One .30-caliber machine gun, two ground mounted .50s and all twenty-eight bazookas in the battalion'.*

However, with a limited combat-power *Kampfgruppe* Jungwirth did not attempt to approach St Oedenrode.

Just after dark, Captain McGlone and 907/GFA's Executive Officer set out to discover what was going on in front of his guns. In the light of a burning tank, they spotted movement ahead of them. This proved not to be the enemy but a British Brigadier, who had been cut-off by the German attack. He had assembled a 'platoon' of 'de-horsed' tank crews, RASC drivers and twelve American Glider Pilots, who had been heading back south. These he had positioned in defensive positions, which had helped to prevent German infantry moving on the screen of Battery B guns in front of St Oedenrode. This was Brigadier Glyn Hughes, who had been sent forward from VIII Corps to find out what was happening, on his Corps' flank as they advanced to the east of Eindhoven.

As darkness set in, grenadiers of Major Jungwirth's *Kampfgruppe* established themselves in the woods astride the road, in all-round defence. Their positions were reinforced, under the cover of darkness, by the arrival of three 88mm guns. However, during the night the Germans were not left to improve their positions unmolested. Again, the Allied artillery blasted their positions, with guns from 7th British Armoured Division (The Desert Rats) and 50th Northumbrian Division joining the shoot, from gun positions south of Eindhoven. Nonetheless, in a SITREP at dawn, Major Jungwirth reported to General Poppe that,

> *'approximately fifty enemy vehicles destroyed and until now eight officers and thirty-two NCOs and men had been captured and sent to the divisional command post'.*

25-26 September 1944 – Allied Counter Attack From The South

During the night, it had become apparent from patrol reports submitted by the 502 PIR and the British 52/Recce Regiment that there were several groups of Allied soldiers holding positions along the line of the road. In some cases they were almost mixed in with the enemy. This meant that it was impractical to use the growing weight of Allied artillery in a decisive manner and that the road would have to be physically cleared. Lieutenant General Horrocks, who had returned south to St Oedenrode to discuss the increasingly bleak prospects for MARKET GARDEN with General Dempsey, promised to help Major General Maxwell Taylor's attack on Koevering from both north and south. The nearest XXX Corps formation was 50th Division, however, with their 69th Brigade already ahead at Nijmegen, and its remaining infantry brigades deployed covering the right flank, they had few troops available. Therefore, 131 (Queen's) Infantry Brigade came under 50th Division's command from 7th Armoured Division along with the tanks of 5/Inniskillen Dragoon Guards (5/Innis DG or the 'Skins') and the 8/Hussars.

The plan was for the Allies to attack north, with 1/502 PIR on the left and 131 Brigade the right of the road. However, the traffic was so bad that the British did not completely assemble until early afternoon. Sergeant Boardman of the 'Skins' recalled the road move:

> *'... the regiment was now under command of the Queen's*

Brigade. The road was packed with vehicles nose to tail unable to move forward or back, but the Military Police, once again, played a wonderful role in sorting it all out. By 07.00 hrs we reached the main square in St Oedenrode where we met a very angry Corps Commander, Lt-Gen Horrocks who was desperately trying to get forward to join his own TAC HQ.'

50th Division, possibly keen to get a bad tempered corps commander out of their Headquarters, volunteered the Durham Light Infantry's Carrier Platoon from 151 Brigade to take him north to The Island. The six carriers, with their precious cargo, took a circuitous route and across country, avoiding contact with the enemy. The General eventually reached his TAC HQ some time after 10.00 hours on 25 September. With Hell's Highway still closed and the previous night's crossing operation a failure, he confirmed that the evacuation of 1st British Airborne would go ahead that night (25 / 26 September).

Meanwhile, at 07.30 hours, with only the leading elements of 131 Brigade having arrived in St Oedenrode, 1/502 PIR, reinforced by Company H and ten tanks from the Guards Armoured Division's Armoured Replacement Squadron, launched an attack north. The Armoured Replacements had been extracted from the traffic jam and sent forward overnight. Staff Sergeant Patheiger, of HQ Company 502 PIR, was with attacking infantry and described what happened:

'Almost immediately, four of the supporting tanks were knocked out by 88mm fire and the company accompanying the tanks were pinned down by small arms fire from automatic weapons and artillery. Four more tanks were brought up to assist the advance, but were put out of action by enemy 88mm fire almost immediately upon getting into position. When the 88mm guns were spotted, friendly troops were so close it was unsafe to bring artillery fire upon them. One 57mm AT gun was brought up and laid on the 88mm gun, which was in a position behind a hedgerow near the road. Several hits were made and it was put out of action. ... In a fire fight that lasted until 18.00 hours, the enemy was pushed back bit by bit.'

131 Brigade were eventually assembled on the northern outskirts of St Oedenrode. The plan was for 1st/7th Queens supported by 5/Inniskilling Dragoon Guards to strike north on the eastern side of the road and join 1/502 PIR at Koevering. At the same time, 8/Hussars supported 1st/5th Queens in a north-

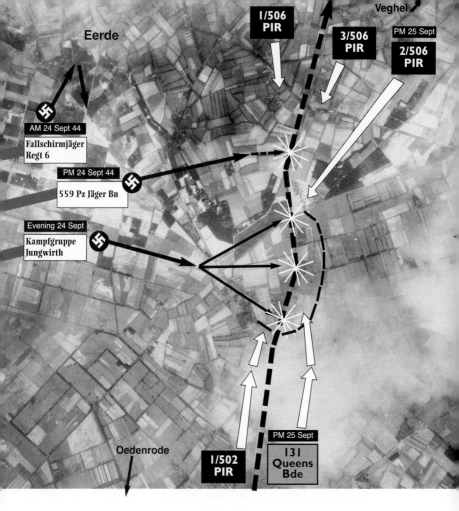

westerly advance to Schijndel. Both advances made slow progress, as at least two 88mm guns were still in position and *Panzerjäger* were repeatedly encountered on the western flank. By late afternoon, 1st/7th Queen's and 5/Innis DG Group had moved into line alongside 1/502 PIR. With sufficient combat power now assembled, significant progress was made against *Kampfgruppe* Jungwirth and a link up was made with 506 PIR to the east of the road. However, in the gathering dusk, C Squadron 5/Innis DG came under fire from American anti-tank guns. With two forces approaching each other from the opposite direction, this incident prompted General Taylor to draw operations to a close for the night. The operations towards

Schijndel mounted by the 1st/5th Queens and 8/Hussars Group, although slow, prevented von der Hydte from responding to Major Jungwirth's appeal for support. Major Jungwirth complained:

> *'The right flank of our left neighbour* [6 Fallschirmjaeger Regiment] *is now at least two kilometres behind. Request action soonest from our left neighbour to restore the link with Koevering.'*

25-26 September 1944 – 506 PIR Attacks From the North

Assembly for the attack south on the night of 24/25 September, required the foot-sore paratroopers to perform yet another counter-march. The 101st's divisional history records

> *'At 0300 the 506th with the 321st* [Artillery] *and Battery B of the 81st was ordered back down from Uden to attack and clear the highway. Moving through the heavy rain of that night, the weary men passed Veghel.'*

While 506 PIR concentrated south of Veghel at 06.00 hours, with the help of 2/HCR's armoured cars; the 101st Airborne's Reconnaissance Platoon had located the enemy positions. According to 44/RTR, they established that,

> *'the enemy were astride the road in battalion strength, with four or five tanks and self-propelled guns and that the road itself was mined'.*

Colonel Sink's plan was simple, with an H Hour of 08.30, 506 PIR attacked south down the road towards Major Jungwirth's *Kampfgruppe* on a narrow two-battalion frontage. The unit after-action report described the initial stages of the battle:

> *'The attack jumped off at 0830 with 3rd Bn leading* [east of the road], *with one-half squadron of tanks attached and 1st Bn following to the right* [west] *rear. 2nd Bn in reserve. At 1130 the 3rd Bn was held up so the 1st Bn was needed to protect the right flank of the regiment ...'*

As indicated by the three hours between H Hour and 11.30 hours, the infantry made slow progress in the early morning mist and rain, which prevented accurate artillery and tank fire support. *Spandaus* and German tanks firing from positions well concealed in the edge of the small woods covered the open ground that the Americans had to cross and brought the attack to a halt. First Lieutenant Andros recalled:

> *'The landscape was very flat and the enemy had some good*

grazing fire set up and you couldn't move over the ground. That grazing fire was really low. The musette bag on my back had the top ripped off by machine gun fire.'

The divisional history recalls how 'The 3rd Battalion had to halt and dig-in, and then the 1st'. Colonel Sink, in the American manouverist style, immediately committed 2/506 PIR and B Squadron 44/RTR to a flanking attack, while 1 and 3/506 kept the German's attention fixed to the north and poured in suppressive fire. An RTR officer recounted that:

'About this time news was received that an unknown armoured column was setting out from St Oedenrode to assist. After a lot of dial-searching we intercepted what was obviously an armoured regiment in full chat, and, breaking in, contact was established with the 8th Hussars, who were identified after a lot of veiled speech and remarks on the colour of various hats. Their plan was to drive north from St Oedenrode towards Schijndel.'

The move of 2/506 PIR and half of B Squadron 44/RTR to the east of the cut at Koevering was slow, as the overnight rain and numerous drainage ditches made difficult going for the tanks. 44/RTR's after action report recorded that:

'B Squadron's leading troop, No. 4, or what was left of it had been halted in their short left hook by multitudes of enemy tanks,

Fallschirmjäger artillery in action. their fire hindered progress on Hell's Highway.

A German self-propelled gun which was knocked out Hell's Highway at Koevering. The gun was a fast firing weapon and was deadly in close quarter engagement.

who appeared from behind every bush. Also halted, were the American parachute infantry, by small-arms fire. The residue, therefore, swung even further to the east and approached the main battle through thick woods, and after a pretty bloody battle in which Sgt Newman and his crew were killed, the road was reached after last light and an infantry link-up took place with the 1st/5th Queen's on the left and with 501 PIR on the right.'

Progress in making this link up to the east of the road was slow, as the British armour was understandably cautious following their encounters with powerful German anti-tank guns. In addition, immediate artillery support to the 506 PIR was limited, due to a lack of ammunition north of the cut. Sergeant Lipton of Company E, 2/506 PIR recalled the fighting:

'When we were in the middle of a very large open area, they opened up on us with small arms, mortars and direct fire from tanks in woods adjacent to the open area. We hit the ground, which was slightly rolling, and gave some cover to the men ... The Sherman tanks were behind us on the minor road and we could see the German positions and three of their tanks on the far side of the field, we yelled to our tanks to come up to fire on them. The British lead tank left the road and came forward through the trees. We were yelling to the commander that the German tanks were right across the field (about 400 yards) and the British tank officer [Sgt Newman] had the hatch open and was standing up with field glasses looking in that direction. For some inexplicable

reason, the British tank continued to move forward until its front pushed out of the wood into the open field.

A 75mm shell from one of the Panthers slammed into the British tank, hitting the shield around its gun without penetrating it. ... The Sherman was open throttle in reverse to back into the woods again but it was too late. The second shell hit below the gun shield and penetrated the armour. The tank commander's hands were blown off and he was trying to get out of the hatch using his arms when the third shell hit the tank blowing him out of the hatch killing him and setting the tank on fire. It burned all night with its ammo exploding at intervals.'

Despite slow progress and setbacks, by 19.40 hours, the link up between 2/506 PIR and 131 Brigade was being reported on the eastern side of the German positions on the highway. As already recorded, General Taylor halted the advance for the night, leaving the enemy in possession of a portion of the road but as Schutze Heinz Sitter of *Kampfgruppe* Jungwirth recalled:

'Dusk. Orders to break out. A march of a few kilometres, then enemy contacts towards dawn. We lie up with Captain Ortmann and a sergeant in a farm house. Enemy artillery pounding us, then come the tanks Next to us is an anti tank gun with a truck full of ammunition, which does not fire a single shot. Apparently a broken firing pin.Tanks are shooting us up with direct fire.'

Hell's Highway Reopened – 26 September 1944

By the following morning the Germans had largely withdrawn to the west and as C Battery 377 Parachute Field Artillery's diary records:

'26 Sept – Weather is very bad with lots of rain falling. "Hell's Highway" still cut but an attack is scheduled for 08.00 hours. Battery has fired quite heavy since early morning in conjunction with coming attack. ... H Company 502 PIR supported by tanks and artillery successfully reopened 'Hell's Highway' at 0930 hours. No traffic is yet allowed to use the road because of 88's zeroed on the road.'

Despite clearing the road of enemy by mid-morning, the route north was by no means open. Firstly, assault guns, were still able to close in on the road and engage anything moving. Secondly, the route was still blocked with the wreckage of over fifty trucks and tanks lost over the preceding days, and thirdly, *Kampfgruppe* Jungwirth had been on the road long enough to liberally sow both anti-tank and anti-personnel mines. The mines and wreckage took the 326 US Engineer Battalion and the Royal Engineers time to clear and XXX Corps' Club Route north was not open until late in the day. However, with the earlier removal of *Kampfgruppe* Walther an alternative route around the cut at Koevering to the east was Tac signed with an Ace of Hearts. This route, however, required significant coordination by 50th Division to bring into use for light vehicles. The route had to be manned by Military Police, while the Royal Engineers had to repair roads and strengthen bridges for sustained traffic.

Aftermath

Once the main route was open and XXX Corps traffic resumed its northward flow, evidence of the fighting was all too obvious to soldiers moving up towards Nijmegen and the Island. Amongst them was Lieutenant Robert Boscawen of the Coldstream Guards. He recorded that:

> *When we moved on through the gap* ['cut'] *the US airborne were still literally dug-in along the ditches on either side of the road prepared for further counter-attacks. The tangled wreckage of our supply vehicles was a sad spectacle, with one of our knocked out Delivery Squadron tanks upside down resting on top of its turret in a field.*

With VIII Corps holding ground to the east and the Grenadier Guards operating to the west, the road was never again cut in significant strength. However, the Germans took every opportunity to raid and disrupt Allied traffic on the road. Private Rex Wingfield of 1/6 Queens wrote of one of these raids:

> *The rest of us mounted on Cromwells turned back to clear the roads. We soon found the targets of last night's firing - ten gutted RASC lorries, one blasted to fragments. That had been the ammo truck. Two hundred yards further down the road was a roadblock of logs. ... A clatter of tracer bounced and sang off the tank as a spandau opened fire from the roadblock. Cordite fumes blasted from our tank gun into our faces. A six-pounder shell hit right in the middle of the logs. The beams sailed upwards. A fieldgrey rag doll jerked high into the air. We burst through, firing Stens and heaving grenades into the smoking roadblock ... Each morning we had to clear the roads in front and behind before we could move on.*

The battle fought by the Guards to break through the German

defences and the Screaming Eagle's marching and counter marching to keep twenty miles of Hell's Highway, open is justifiably one of the Northwest European Campaign's most celebrated battles. The 101st Airborne and the Guards Armoured Divisions fought together heroically, supported by the West Countrymen of 231 Brigade and other British armoured units. These very different formations, faced odds that, if fully realized by Montgomery's MARKET GARDEN planners in early September, would have been considered impossible. In the final analysis it must be concluded that the delay imposed by the blowing of the Son Bridge and the other cuts to the route north was to have a profound effect on the operations of British and American divisions at Nijmegen and on The Island.

The battles to the north are covered in separate Battleground Europe volumes that follow the entire MARKET GARDEN Campaign. *Battleground Nijmegen* covers the fighting by 82nd US Airborne and the Guards to capture the Maas/Waal bridges and hold the Groesbeek heights. *Battleground The Island* covers the Guards attempt to reach Arnhem, 43rd Wessex Division's advance to reinforce the 1st Airborne Division at Oosterbeek and the eventual evacuation of the British paratroopers.

To follow Hell's Highway north, take the **N265** back to **Veghel** and **Uden**. Turn right onto the **N321** towards **Grave**. The **Battleground Nijmegen** tour starts at the bridge over the Mass just beyond Grave.

The Eerde Windmill and 501 PIR's memorial.

201

APPENDIX I

THE CLOSURE OF CLUB ROUTE / HELL'S HIGHWAY BY ENEMY ACTION

'The line of communication must be certain and well established, for every army that acts from a distant base and is not careful to keep this line perfectly open marches upon a precipice. It moves to certain ruin if the road by which provisions, ammunition, and reinforcements are to be brought up is not entirely secured.'

Raimundo Montecuccoli
(1609 - 80)
Memoroe della guerra ed instruzione d'un general
(Venice 1703)

Much of the criticism of XXX Corps during MARKET GARDEN is based on a lack of understanding of the impact of a cut in an armoured or mechanised formation's lines of communication. Also, airborne forces are, expected to conduct most of their operations behind enemy lines and are therefore familiar with the idea of being 'cut off' and sustained for short periods by air. Many of XXX Corps' critics have failed to appreciate the quantity of combat supplies required by a corps conducting offensive operations. By the time the spearhead of XXX Corps had reached Nijmegen, its logistic vehicles were operating at distances of seventy miles from their combat supplies Distribution Points, located between the Albert and Escaut Canals. The round trip of one hundred and forty miles was complicated not only by the cuts but also by the need to close the route to returning traffic, in favour of urgently needed formations moving forward. XXX Corps was operating on a single 'Centre Line' or axis and was, therefore, extremely vulnerable to enemy action. Traffic prioritization was not good but the problem was exacerbated by the need to get the 'Sea Tail' (the supply vehicles) of the three airborne divisions forward as a priority.

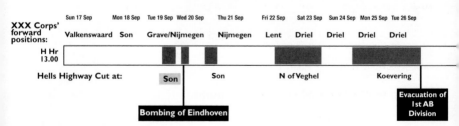

APPENDIX II

ORDERS OF BATTLE

GUARDS ARMOURED DIVISION

The Guards Armoured Division had by September 1944 departed from its official ORBAT to form, uniquely, regimental groups of armour and infantry that habitually fought together. This closeness, unusual at the time, between the two arms brought many benefits. However, their critics also, with little solid evidence, use this grouping to attribute a certain ponderousness to the Division.

HQ GUARDS ARMOURED DIVISION

Guards Armoured Division Signal Regiment (-)

HQ 5th GUARDS ARMOURED BRIGADE ('Group Hot')

1st (Motorized) Battalion, The Grenadier Guards
2nd (Armoured) Battalion, The Grenadier Guards
1st (Armoured) Battalion, The Coldstream Guards
5th Battalion, The Coldstream Guards
55th Field Regiment Royal Artillery
14th Field Squadron Royal Engineers

HQ 32nd GUARDS ARMOURED BRIGADE ('Group Cold')

2nd (Armoured) Battalion, The Irish Guards
3rd Battalion, The Irish Guards
1st Battalion, The Welsh Guards
2nd (Armoured Recconnisance) Battalion,
The Welsh Guards
153rd (Leicestershire Yeomanry) Field Regiment Royal Artillery
615th Field Squadron Royal Engineers

GUARDS ARMOURED DIVISIONAL TROOPS

HQ 21st Anti-Tank Regiment Royal Artillery
HQ 94th Light Anti-Aircraft Regiment Royal Artillery
HQ Guards Armoured Division Engineer Regiment, Field Park Company 11th Bridging Troop RE and Divisional Postal Unit
Number 1 Independent Machinegun Company, The Royal Northumberland Fusiliers
Royal Army Service Corps
HQ Guards Armoured Division RASC Battalion, Tank Delivery Squadron
Royal Army Medical Corps
19th Light Field Ambulance, 128th Field Ambulance and Field Hygiene Section
Royal Army Ordnance Corps Guards Armoured Division 0rdnance Field Park, Company RAOC and Mobile Bath Unit
Royal Electrical and Mechanical Engineers   5th Guards Armoured Brigade Workshop, 32nd Guards Armoured Brigade Workshop
Military Police Guards Armoured Division Company Royal Corps of Military Police
Intelligence Corps Field Security Section

231st (MALTA) INFANTRY BRIGADE

2nd Battalion, The Devonshire Regiment
1st Battalion, The Dorsetshire Regiment
1st Battalion, The Hampshire Regiment
90th Field Regiment Royal Artillery

DETACHMENT 4th ARMOURED BRIGADE
>44th Royal Tank Regiment (to 101st Airborne Division)

DETACHMENT 11th ARMOURED DIVISION
>5th / 19th Hussars (to 231 Brigade and subsequently to 101st Airborne Division)

101st US AIRBORNE DIVISION

HEADQUARTERS 101ST US AIRBORNE DIVISION
>101st Signal Company and 101st Headquarter Company

501st PARACHUTE INFANTRY REGIMENT
>1st Battalion, 501st Parachute Infantry Regiment
>2nd Battalion, 501st Parachute Infantry Regiment
>3rd Battalion, 501st Parachute Infantry Regiment

502nd PARACHUTE INFANTRY REGIMENT
>1st Battalion, 502nd Parachute Infantry Regiment
>2nd Battalion, 502nd Parachute Infantry Regiment
>3rd Battalion, 502nd Parachute Infantry Regiment

506th PARACHUTE INFANTRY REGIMENT
>1st Battalion, 506th Parachute Infantry Regiment
>2nd Battalion, 506th Parachute Infantry Regiment
>3rd Battalion, 506th Parachute Infantry Regiment

327th GLIDER INFANTRY REGIMENT
>1st Battalion, 327th Glider Infantry Regiment
>2nd Battalion, 327th Glider Infantry Regiment
>1st Battalion, 401st Glider Infantry Regiment

DIVISIONAL TROOPS
>101st Parachute Maintenance Battalion
>326th Airborne Engineer Battalion
>326th Airborne Medical Company Attached Field Hospital
>81st Airborne Anti-aircraft and Anti-tank Battalion
>321st Glider Field Artillery Battalion
>377th Parachute Field Artillery Battalion
>907th Glider Field Artillery Battalion
>801st Ordnance Company
>426th Quartermaster Company
>397th Quartermaster Truck Company
>101st Military Police Platoon
>101st Reconnaissance Platoon

APPENDIX III
CEMETERIES

The MARKET GARDEN Graves

The soldiers of all nations who took part in MARKET GARDEN and were killed in action or died of wounds are now widely spread across Europe, Britain and the USA. However, a significant number still lie on cemeteries on or near the battlefields covered by this book. This annex contains details of the cemeteries and how to find them.

The Commonwealth War Graves Commission (CWGC)

The Commonwealth War Commission was formed in 1917, originally as the Imperial War Graves Commission, under Major General Sir Fabian Ware. As commander of a Red Cross mobile unit Ware started to record names and locations of graves, which at the time, beyond a wooden cross went largely unrecorded despite Army regulations. Good intentions, however, broke down in the chaos and under the weight of casualties. Under pressure from home, the War Office approved the formation of a Graves Registration Unit in 1915, under Ware who became a Temporary Major. Gradually the importance of care of war graves grew and in 1917 the present organization was founded. Today the Commission works in 140 countries and tends 1,146,105 graves and maintains memorials to many thousands more Commonwealth Soldiers who lost their lives in the Twentieth Century. General Haig commented in 1915:

> 'It is recognized that the work of the organization is of purely sentimental value, and that it does not directly contribute to the successful termination of the war. It has, however, an extraordinary moral value to the troops as well as to the relatives and friends of the dead at home... Further, on the termination of hostilities, the nation will demand an account from the government as to the steps which have been taken to mark and classify the burial places of the dead...'

CWGC Cemetery Leopoldsburg

This cemetery is hard to find, as it is located off the main N73 road, on the outskirts of a Belgian Army Garrison near Leopoldsburg and is poorly signed. There are 767 graves, many of which are from the period of the advance from Brussels to the Escaut Canal, which culminated in the seizure of Joe's bridge. Other graves date from later in the campaign, when a field hospital was located in the nearby barracks.

CWGC Cemetery Valkenswaard

This small woodland cemetery is located on the N69 between Joe's Bridge and Valkenswaard itself. The cemetery was originally formed by the Irish Guards for the burial of soldiers killed on the opening day of MARKKET GARDEN. There are 222 British soldiers and two airmen, of whom thirty were killed on 17 or 18 September. The largest single regimental representation is the sixteen Irish Guardsmen killed during the breakout. They are buried very close to where they died in the German tank ambush on that Sunday afternoon. Also heavily represented are 2/Devons of 231 Brigade with eleven graves. These soldiers were killed while clearing the enemy from the surrounding woods as they advanced, on foot, parallel to the road. The remainder of the graves are mainly from the MARKET GARDEN period but are not exclusively from XXX Corps.

CWGC Eindhoven Woensel Civilian Cemetery

Having just turned off the Eindhoven inner ring road onto the John F Kennedy road keep an eye open for the green and white CWGC sign, on the left, indicating the Wonsel Cemetery. The CWGC plot containing 666 burials is an extension of the civilian cemetery

CWGC Cemetery Uden

699 burials. the cemetery is signed from N265 Uden bypass. A high proportion of the burials date from the MARKET GARDEN period.

American Battle Monuments Commission

Similar to the Commonwealth War Graves Commission, the American Battle Monuments Commission (ABMC) is an agency of the Executive Branch of the US federal government. It is responsible for commemorating the service of US Forces' world wide since April 1917 (their entry into World War I) by establishing suitable memorials and constructing, operating and maintaining permanent American military cemeteries overseas. The ABMC is also responsible for controlling the design and construction of U.S. military monuments and markers in foreign countries erected by other US citizens and organizations, both public and private; and overseeing their maintenance.

In 1947, the US Congress decided to give next of kin the option to chose where they would like the serviceman to be buried (unlike the Commonwealth next of kin). The choices were to remain in the theatre where they died or to return them to the US for burial in National Military Cemeteries or under private arrangements in hometown cemeteries. About 63% of all bodies were repatriated during 1948 and 1949.

The remaining US military graves were concentrated into a few large cemeteries. Of the 320,423 Second World War bodies of US servicemen, the ABMC is responsible for 93,242 graves across the world. The remainder of the bodies were returned to their families. Also commemorated by the ABMC are the names of 78,976 soldiers who are listed as Missing in Action.

Margraten Cemetery

Margraten is the only ABMC cemetery in Holland. The dead who were to remain in the care of the ABMC were brought here from temporary cemeteries across Holland, such as that at Mollenhoek at the foot of the Grossbeck heights. The cemetery is situated in the village of Margraten, six miles east of Maastricht near the southernmost point of Holland some two hours drive south of Nijmegen. The Cemetery is well signposted.

Margarten's tall memorial tower is clearly visible as the visitor approaches the site, which covers over sixty acres. From the cemetery entrance, the visitor enters the Court of Honour with its pool reflecting the tower. To the right and left, respectively, are the visitors' building and a building containing on its walls three engraved maps showing the operations conducted by US Forces in 1944 and 1945. Stretching along the side of the Court are the two Walls of the Missing on which are recorded the names of 1,723 who gave their lives in the service of the USA but who rest in unknown graves. At the base of the tower, facing the reflecting pool is a statue representing the grieving mother of her lost son. Beyond the tower, containing the cemetery's chapel is the burial area. Divided into 16 plots the cemetery contains 8,301 graves, with the headstones set in long curves. A wide tree-lined mall leads to the flagstaff.

In the summer, the cemetery is open to visitors daily from 09.00 - 18.00 hours and in the winter from 09.00 to 17.00 hours. Details of the ABMC its work and cemeteries can be found on the Internet on http://www.usabmc.com/index.shtml

German

The German MARKET GARDEN dead are widely spread in cemeteries across the border in Germany or in the German Deutsche Kriegsgrabefürsorge cemetery at Lommel near Joe's Bridge in Belgium or in Holland at Ijsselstijn.

Lommel German Cemetery

Turn left in, at the cross roads before reaching Joe's Bridge. Head towards Hasselt and follow the white signs with black text 'Deutscher Soldaten Friedhof' to the cemetery. Originally an American temporary cemetery, this attractively laid out cemetery contains 542 graves dating back to the First World War. In 1947,once the American dead had been repatriated, no less than 38,614 German bodies were concentrated here from four other cemeteries in Belgium.

Ijsselstijn German Cemetery

Ijsselstijn German War Cemetery is sited in a remote spot thirty kilometres west of Eindhoven between that city and Venray. Follow the A270 from Eindhoven to Helmond where the road turns into the N270. Continue until the junction with the N277 is reached. Ijsseltijn is a mile to the south on the N277.

German soldiers who died and were originally buried in Holland between 1940 and 1945, were disinterred after the war and moved from communal or battlefield cemeteries across Holland and concentrated here for reburial. There are 31,511 bodies interned in this cemetery. Many of the soldiers who lie here, are those of the 8,000 (approximately) Germans killed during Operation MARKET GARDEN. Those from II SS Panzer Corps killed in Arnhem and on the Island were originally buried in the SS Heroes Cemetery on the outskirts of Arnhem. In line with normal policy, SS ranks have been converted into their Wehrmacht equivalents on all graves and memorials.

INDEX